MUD CLOTH ROOTS

STRAIGHT OUT SCRIBES

DR. V.S. CHOCHEZI AND STAAJABU

Copyright © 2015 Dr. V.S. Chochezi and Staajabu

All rights reserved.

Photos by Jessicah Ciel

Greetings, acknowledgements and livecation

This is our 25th Anniversary year of being a writing, publishing, performing poetry team, in partnership, as co-authors and co-producers. We are Straight Out Scribes, Dr. V.S. Chochezi, daughter and Staajabu, mother and founder. To celebrate our long, productive and successful alliance and to pay tribute to our ancestors, family, friends and fans, we offer this new collection, a total of 102 original poems (51 each) written by the two of us. We thank all of you for your support through the years. As we continue to grow as a family, Straight Out Scribes will continue writing, producing, creating, sharing, caring and enjoying the gift of poetry while simultaneously educating, inspiring and encouraging people to use the awesome power of their minds to bring about positive change that will benefit our planet.

This book is livecated foremost to our family in Brotmanville, Vineland, Newfield, Camden and Sicklerville NJ; Philadelphia, PA,;Warner Robins, Macon and Locust Grove, GA; Kansas City, MO; Toledo, OH; Jacksonville, FL; and Galt, Sacramento, and Stockton, CA.

We acknowledge all the great poets/writers/seers and knowers who joined the ancestors since our last publication. May their legacies live on in our hearts and minds forever.

We acknowledge the passing of Rev. Dr. Isiah Woods, Chochezi's father who joined the ancestors in November 2014. The best of all his talents and gifts live on in his children, grandchildren and great grandchildren. He touched the lives of many and is sorely missed. We also acknowledge and welcome the addition of Makhai, Saje, Isaias and Billy Ward to the Sacramento Scribe tribe.

Much respect to Assata Shakur, THE MOVE FAMILY AFRICA, Brotha Mumia Abu-Jamal, Leonard Peltier, Mondo Eyen we Langa and all political prisoners who refused to compromise their belief in what is right and just and are paying the price with the loss of their freedom.

If you find this work to be in any way beneficial, educational, inspiring, thought provoking or fun, all Praise is due to the Most High Creative Energy in the Universe.

Mud Cloth Roots *"A tree is strong because of its roots" – African Proverb*

In the West African country of Mali, the word "bògòlanfini" in the Bambara language is a composite of bogo, meaning "earth" or "mud"; *lan*, meaning "with" or "by means of"; and *fini*, meaning "cloth" and translates to "mud cloth."

We are certain that our ancestors originated in Africa though we have no physical or documented proof. A majority of those ancestors seem to have come from West Africa according to the sea routes that depict the waterways traveled by the traders of humans from Africa to North America, South America, the Caribbean and Europe. You might say the mud cloth called to us because as soon as we saw garments made from it we were immediately attracted to it. We felt its significance before we even knew what it was called. When contemplating the title of this, our seventh book of poetry, we scribes knew mud cloth would be a part of it. It is a part of our heritage or roots and the ancient complicated process of producing this cloth from all natural sources (cotton, tree roots, mud, millet, sunlight and palm fronds) mirrored our struggle and growth as writers and poets who by example and productivity, have passed the tradition on to the youth in our family and community.

Mud is the essence of the dye which makes the design on the cloth. Mud is a mix of earth and water, both elements essential to life and growth. Straight Out Scribes, have woven our own symbolic mud cloth from digging deep into the mud of our souls and mixing it with the spirits of our ancestors, the lessons of our elders and the promise of our youth to produce this, our seventh offering of original writings in celebration of the twenty-fifth year of our journey together as a mother/daughter poetry team.

There's a strong mother/daughter connection in the Bogolanfini or mud cloth. Traditionally, Bambara (Bamana) women, as well as those of the Minianka, Senufo, Dogon, and other ethnic groups in Mali produced the cloth for important life events and taught the process to their daughters. Mud cloth patterns are not only decorative, they also have symbolic meanings.

These designs are handed from mother to daughter during their apprenticeship. Traditionally, women were wrapped in mud cloth after their initiation into adulthood and immediately after childbirth, as the cloth was believed to have the power to absorb the dangerous forces released under such circumstances.

Mud cloth in Africa dates as far back as the 12th century AD. The symbols and shape arrangement on the mud cloth reveals a variety of different meanings. Today, both women and men make mud cloth for sale in markets, and Malian students study it at the arts academy.

References

Donne, J.B. (1973). "Bogolanfini: A Mud-Painted Cloth from Mali". **8** (1). JSTOR

The Free Encyclopedia, 19 Aug. 2014. Web. 19 Jan. 2015.

Hager, Liz (March 1, 2010). "Malian Bogolanfini and Cultural Identity." *Venetian Red*.

Hilu, Sam; Hersey, Irwin (2005). *Bogolanfini Mud Cloth*. Atglen, Pa.: Schiffer Publishing Ltd. ISBN 978-0-7643-2187-0.

Imperato, Pascal James; Shamir, Marli (1970). "Bokolanfini: Mud Cloth of the Bamana of Mali". *African Arts* **3** (4): 32–41, 80. doi:10.2307/3345905.

Rovine, Victoria (1997). "Bogolanfini in Bamako: The Biography of a Malian Textile". *African Arts* **30** (1): 40–51+9496. JSTOR 3337471.

Rovine, Victoria L. (2005). "Bogolan". In Steele, Valerie. *Encyclopedia of Clothing and Fashion* **1**. Thomson Gale. pp. 149–150. ISBN 0-684-31394-4.

Toerien, Elsje S (2003). "Mud cloth from Mali: its making and use". *Journal of Family Ecology and Consumer Sciences* **31**: 52–57. ISSN 0378-5254.

CONTENTS

Chapter I: Popular Pursuits - Shughuli Maarufu – Búsquedas Populares

Poem	Author	Page
A hint of recognition	V.S. Chochezi	11
Caution	V.S. Chochezi	13
Corner bar	Staajabu	15
Lingering	Staajabu	17
Renewed acquaintance I	Staajabu	18
Traps	V.S. Chochezi	19
Sheep like	Staajabu	20
Condolences for my sistahs	Staajabu	21
Third floor front	Staajabu	22
In the zone	V.S. Chochezi	24
Mind speak	Staajabu	25
Old school	Staaajabu	26
Farm worker woman	V.S. Chochezi	27
Jobs I've had	Staajabu	29
Keeping it real	V.S. Chochezi	30
I live with HIV now	Staajabu	31
Where there was once ocean	V.S. Chochezi	33
Now what?	V.S. Chochezi	34
One shoe	Staajabu	35
By the numbers	Staajabu	37
Hunger	V.S. Chochezi	39
Patchouli anyone?	Staajabu	40
Another day	Staajabu	41
The long haul	V.S. Chochezi	42
Don't hate	V.S. Chochezi	44
Woman's work	Staajabu	46

Chapter 2: Viewpoints – Maoni – Puntos de Vista

Poem	Author	Page
Resist	Staajabu	49
Next best revolutionary	V.S. Chochezi	50
Run	Staajabu	52
How do you expect me	V.S. Chochezi	53
Power to the people	Staajabu	55
Governments play war games	V.S. Chochezi	56
Recaptured splendor	V.S. Chochezi	58
Battles to be fought	Staajabu	60
The message	Staajabu	61
They should	V.S. Chochezi	62
Back of the bus	Staajabu	64
Excuse me?	V.S. Chochezi	65
How do they oppress us?	Staajabu	67
Pieces lost	Staajabu	69
An eye for an eye	Staajabu	71
Undying faith	V.S. Chochezi	72
Reparations illustration	Staajabu	75

Chapter 3: Love – Upendo – Amor

Poem	Author	Page
Black man	Staajabu	77
Love sphere	V.S. Chochezi	78
Met her at low tide	V.S. Chochezi	80
Clean love	Staajabu	81
Swooning	V.S. Chochezi	82
Don't be fooled	V.S. Chochezi	83
Love that, that will love you back	Staajabu	85
Love and romance	V.S. Chochezi	86
Dancing in the junk	Staajabu	89
Prisoner of love	Staajabu	90
About love	V.S. Chochezi	91
Chemical reaction	V.S. Chochezi	94
Giving thanks and praises	Staajabu	95

Chapter 4: Poetry and Words – Mashairi na Maneno – Poesia y Palabras

Poem	Author	Page
Joyful abandon	V.S. Chochezi	97
Poetry is my thang	Staajabu	98
Blank page	V.S. Chochezi	99
Pain is	Staajabu	101
Poets are going to poet	V.S. Chochezi	102
Slam poets	Staajabu	103
Words	V.S. Chochezi	104
Tumbling inside out	Staajabu	106

Chapter 5: Cosmic Routes – Nija Cosmic – Rutas Cósmicas

Poem	Author	Page
Prayer for the planet	Staajabu	108
Theoretically speaking	V.S. Chochezi	109
Spirit voices	V.S. Chochezi	110
Coming into over-standing	Staajabu	112
Forgotten truths	V.S. Chochezi	113
Empowered	V.S. Chochezi	114
No loss to grieve	V.S. Chochezi	115
Upon further reflection	V.S. Chochezi	117
Many paths	V.S. Chochezi	118
Peace	Staajabu	121

Chapter 6: Natural Sense – Maana ya Asili – Sentido Natural

Poem	Author	Page
If you could just hear	V.S. Chochezi	124
Mama ocean beckons	V.S. Chochezi	126
Special effects	Staajabu	127
Tree stories	V.S. Chochezi	128
Angels camp	V.S. Chochezi	129
Making snow sense	Staajabu	131
Early mosaic reflection	V.S. Chochezi	132
Great snack	V.S. Chochezi	133
Hell No to GMOs	V.S. Chochezi	134
Herd of elephants symphony	V.S. Chochezi	135
Renewed acquaintance II	Staajabu	136

Chapter 7: Recognition and Respect – Utambuzi na Heshima – Reconocimiento y Respeto

Poem	Author	Page
I wish you well	Staajabu	138
Mommy look!	Staajabu	139
Far above the surface	V.S. Chochezi	140
When my daughter smiles	Staajabu	141
Captivated	V.S. Chochezi	142
A beautiful line	Staajabu	143
Tribute to reggae	Staajabu	145
The griot	Staajabu	146
Dancing with Saleem	Staajabu	147
Just musing	V.S. Chochezi	148
To sisterhood	V.S. Chochezi	149
Elizabeth Catlett tribute	V.S. Chochezi	151
Rag time	V.S. Chochezi	152
Honoring Chinua Achebe	V.S. Chochezi	154
Meditation for Maya Angelou	Staajabu	155
Rev. Dr. Martin Luther King, Jr.	V.S. Chochezi	156
Mzaliwa home	V.S. Chochezi	157
Thanks for the music	Staajabu	158
Fierce!	Staajabu	159

Chapter I

Popular Pursuits

Shughuli Maarufu

Búsquedas Populares

A hint of recognition

Ethiopians knit their brow
Jamaicans do a double take
Native Americans give
A knowing nod
Nigerians often seem certain
South Africans cock the head
To one side, squint their eyes and sigh
African-Americans look quizzically

Perhaps it's the locs crowning the head
The ankh in the earlobe or around the neck
The red, black, green and gold bracelets
The Marley T-shirt
The thick lips, gapped teeth highlighted
By a bright smile
The mud cloth and the
Gye Nyame on the outfit

The accents — Jersey mixed with Valley
Sprinkled with Puerto Rican
Influenced Spanish
Matriarch, strong back,
Straight neck, sure foot
That catches the eye and
Captures the imagination

The double chocolate
Caramel coated
Cinnamon toasted
Burnt custard hues
Or a little something extra
In the attitude

Don't get it twisted
It's not about a wannabe
Because even the stiff straight
Preacher, one generation before
In black robe and white collar
Who speaks only North Carolina

Tinged English and knows a few
Words in KiSwahili would be
Difficult to distinguish from
Several Nigerian brothers we know

See we don't suffer from
Identity confusion
It's an unmistakable resemblance
The true testimony that shows
While we can't pinpoint
The exact location
Yes, we're clearly related
Solidly connected
Long lost separated coast to coast
Born here or across the sea
Africans are who we be

V.S. Chochezi

Caution

Late for the game, a TV show, work
A true emergency like realizing
You left the stove on
Panic like trying to get to the hospital
To see an injured child
Or get there before the baby is born
Or maybe just impatience

Whatever the issue
Whatever the reason
Careening down the street
Or the freeway swerving
In and out of traffic

Following the bumper ahead
So close that not even a
Shadow could get between
Is not just stupid
Not just dangerous
It's oxymoronic

It's a poor gamble
The odds against success
So high the consequences
Of failure so extreme
Hurrying to a dastardly demise

No room for error
When a tire blows
Or a truck brakes suddenly ahead
Or a car crosses into the blind spot
Of a fellow traveler

There's no time for correction
Perhaps no opportunity for
A second chance
For even a great defensive driver
To avoid the crunch

The splat, a mangled mess
Of machine and flesh
Brings not just the hyper
Motivated motorist to a
Screeching halt

But half the city as traffic
Backs up in both directions
And why is it always at rush hour
On the freezeway?

Breathe. Pause. Ask the question.
Life or death?
Life? Or death?

Is it truly a life or death
Destination that requires
Rushing and swerving
Provoking road rage
And tempting the grim reaper?

Ask the question.
Now, can't we agree
On better late than never?
And proceed with caution?

V.S. Chochezi

Corner bar

I've spent a lot of time in bars
My dad would take me to bars with him
While he sold his corn whiskey to
Bartenders and bar owners
He would sit me up high on the bar
And my legs would dangle down
Between barstools
The sound of tinkling glass
The smell of whiskey and smoke
Aftershave and musk kept me
Still and quiet as the men
Admired me and told daddy how
Much I favored him

My mom would take me to the
Corner bar when she and my daddy
Were on the outs and we would
Drink sodas and listen to the
Sad bluesy broken heart lost
Love down and out lamentations
From the bright shiny juke box that would
Come alive magically with the plunk of
A quarter and we would go home with
New resolve to relocate, start anew or
Quit that job but forget it all and go
To bed knowing tomorrow would
Offer many other opportunities

Started going to bars alone or with friends
When I was twelve to play the numbers
Or get a pack of cigarettes
For one of the neighbors
The regulars knew I was Grace's daughter
And D.P was my daddy they'd buy me a soda
Later in my teens I'd
Sneak into The Dew Drop Inn, Tippin' Inn, the
Cotton Club in Lawnside then
After 21 get my dance groove on at
The Square Club in Dover, DE

The Place in Riverside, CA
Smalls Paradise in San Berdoo
The Whiskey A-Go-Go on Sunset Strip
The Democrat Club; 7th & Kaighn
And the Top Hat in Camden, NJ
Buddies Bar in Philly
Ida and Mickey's in Vineland, NJ
Married a man who
Was a blues singer we spent week-ends in bars
Him singing, me drinking, the more I drank
The better he'd sound
I've been kicked out of bars, chased
Out of bars, cowered in corners while
Mayhem broke out all around me
Met lovers, made friends, danced and
Danced for hours on end, listened to
Many a sad sad tale, worked in a Speak
Easy, gotten totally wasted, started
Fights, ran from fights, raids, police,
Pissed off husbands and wives
Watched lives entwine folks unwind and
Come alive in corner bars, pubs, clubs
All over the country…

You know I was in a bar
For the first time in a long time recently
And as soon as I stepped inside
Inhaled the familiar, heard the tinkling
Of ice in a glass, I relaxed, felt right at home
And very, very thirsty.

Staajabu

Lingering

Would you invite two thugs into your house
Listen to their foul mouths
Watch them smoke crack
Abuse each other and their women
In front of your children?

Lingering

Would you invite two lovers
Into your living room
To stroke and kiss and
Do all the things that lovers do
In front of your children
In front of you?

Lingering

When you turn off the TV do the images
Cease to be?

Lingering
Lingering

Staajabu

Renewed acquaintance I

You don't know me
And I might look strange to you
Wearing the clothes that I wear
Hair dread up all over my head and do
Come over here and let me tap on your ear
A second or two a second or two is
All I need for you to feel these
Heed these words while you
Gamin' playin' skippin' and dippin'
Yall need to stop illin just chillin'
Jiving straight trippin'
Stop being small hangin' out at the mall
Watchin' TV and all while your communities fall and
They're trying to kill Mumia Abu-Jamal
You've got skill got talent, got intelligence
So why don't you stand tall and represent
Don't act like a fool who's never been through the
Schools of life, don't know the rules of life—Cool.

Maybe you weren't born to be a king or a queen
But you know you were born to
Be someone crucial on this scene
Respect the people in life
That's got your back in life
Who won't punk out when you're
Under attack in life
Hold your head high open your third eye
And recognize, recognize, recognize
That your mission and your purpose here
Can only succeed with your brothers
And sisters at your side
Let's start respecting one another
Let's start respecting one another
You don't know me
Know me
Know me, and know this
I am your sis-tah

Staajabu

Traps

1. Fear
We crouch and prepare for aliens
Natural catastrophes, police brutality,
Imprisonment and execution of the death penalty

We remain our own worst enemy
Poisoning our chemical sensitive bodies with
Salt, sugar, preservatives and nicotine
Sure to kill us painfully but slooowly

2. Lies
We eat them up like nourishment
Shrouding ourselves in fantasy
Violence, sex and comedy
From every medium imaginable

Games, movies and tv
Sedentary lifestyles preventing
Proper circulation

3. Negativity
Financial disaster and the end of the world
Eat at us until we succumb to cancer
High blood pressure, drug addiction

Diabetes, unfulfilling, lying cheating improper,
Perverted sexual escapades, exploitation and HIV
Stressful existence sure to kill us sooner or later

4. Escape
Ascending in need of higher consciousness
We struggle to avoid the divide and conquer
Tactics that destroyed us in the past
And that continue to work against us

We seek and hope to achieve one love and unity
And free ourselves from the traps.

V.S. Chochezi

Sheep like

Sheep-like people peep through
Bars of their homes, prisons, offices
Cars, holes in doors, curtains, blinds
Trees and bushes searching for more
Of something unnamed

They squint through bus windows occluded
With grainy ads slapped on the side while playing
Hide and seek from a life too much
Of a grainy maze to navigate
But wanting more

Sheep-like people in herds follow lines to graze
On commodities of canned corn and peas
That nobody wants or needs but still must eat
Because like good sheep they do what they are
Told by magazines newspapers and TV
Then ask for more

Peeking through thoughts cluttered with
Subliminal billboards slapped upside their heads
To keep them dead on their feet like
All good meat for the fodder and the
Fatter they get the more they feel
They are fulfilling their own destiny
Peeking, pecking, picking, packing
It in while parking their hypnotized
Mesmerized super sized homogenized
Nutrition starved selves
Into many and sundry too small spaces
Uttering bah bah fat sheep have you any
Have you any, have you any…
More?

Staajabu

Condolences for my sisters
(who never stood a chance)

I offer my sincere condolences
My sisters for the death of your spirit
Murdered by the shampoo and hair
Color commercials that seduced
You into applying chemicals
To the beautiful unruly hair
Which crowned your brilliant, curious mind
I watched you being hindered in your natural
Development by curtailing your activities
To keep your hair intact and Venus forbid
That you should sweat it back, mess it up or have
Some of your roots show, OH NO!!!!!!!
I witnessed your spirit being subdued
By men who wanted you to be quiet at their side
While they made believe they were controlling the world,
Bragging and boasting of their conquests over others, over
Our Mother Earth, keeping you ignorant of your moon cycle

My sympathy sisters for the agony
You endured as you lost your hair
Along with your backbone and in its place
Gained the symptoms of capitalism
Dissatisfaction, greed, vanity, envy
Obesity, apathy, arthritis, diabetes
You never stood a chance because romance
Was fed to you with your first spoon of sugar-laden
Baby food along with stories of punk Cinderella who
Wouldn't stand up for herself, waiting for a prince to save her
Snow dub-ya who fell for the old apple trick
Waiting for a prince to save her
Sleeping' ugly, waiting for a prince to save her
Now here you are watching TV, movies
Reading romance novels and magazines
Waiting for some joker named Botox to save you
My condolences sisters; you never stood a chance.

Staajabu

Third floor front

Third floor front, fifth from the right
You could see my window
From the road as soon as you turned the
Corner after you passed the church and I
Could see for miles from my window the
Big sprawling grounds of our apartment building
Beautifully landscaped with a gazebo
And walkways spiking out in all directions
Encircled by woods gone wild
Big old pines and evergreens.
Wow you do have a gorgeous view
Visitors would say and oh how I enjoyed
Watching the New Jersey seasons
Come and go in this small country town
Where there were only a few buildings as
High and I could see the sky, the lawns
Skunk, deer, foxes, ground hogs, birds
Butterflies the maintenance people doing
Their jobs, the landscapers keeping everything tight
Mr. Sam in his motorized scooter zipping around
The grounds as our self-appointed security guard,
He'd retired from the navy and a car accident
Put a crimp in his style, as he would say.
Sam the Man had outgrown the scooter
A lot of him spilled over in all directions
He kept a big stogy of a cigar
Clamped in the corner of his mouth
And ready joke on his lips. He knew every tenant.
"What the monkey say when they cut off his tail?"
He'd yell when he'd roll on the shopping bus
Then he'd laugh and answer his own question
"It won't be long now." And every one would laugh.
For some reason this never got old and soon
Everyone would join in each time
And each say with their own reason in mind
"It won't be long now."
I'd sit at my window most days and watch
People taking walks, going to the bus stop
Sitting in the gazebo talking about

Everything under the sun, but mostly God
Saw the leaves turn brilliant in the fall and
The first snow flurries of winter.
Watched spring ease her way in with
Light green tenderness and summer wallop us
With sweltering rich deep forest thickness
Saw the handicap bus, the senior center bus
The church bus that took us grocery shopping
The taxi cabs, grown children and grandchildren
Coming and going. Saw ambulances
Taking my neighbors to emergency rooms
Who fell down, suffered a stroke, heart attack
Blood sugar too low, blood pressure too high
Attempted suicides
Saw police cars called by neighbors who were
Losing it and being chased or harassed by their
own selves but trying their best to maintain
Some semblance of independence as they
Grew feeble in mind and body, some
Couldn't hear worth a damn, some couldn't' see
Forgot to take their medications
Wandered off forgot where they lived only
To be brought back to wander off again
Saw neighbors leave never to return
Like Mrs. Washington, Mr. Shearer, Mr. Bill,
Mr. Tom, Ms. Betty, Marcos, Ms. Louise, Ms. Lucille
I do miss the view some days watching
Mother Nature share her bountiful array of
Weather antics; lightening, thunder, black storm
Clouds, snowflakes, hail, drizzle, sleet, rain, fog
The parking lot visited by snowplows, salt trucks
Garbage trucks, mail truck, pharmacy delivery
Moving vans, meals on wheels, visiting nurses
Rent a Center (RAC) trucks, United Parcel
Federal Express, Verizon Wireless, Pest control
All from my third floor front
Fifth from the right window
At Christ Care Senior Housing
In Sicklerville, New Jersey
Known by most as CCU

Staajabu

In the zone

Noses pressed together
The happy, innocent gaze
Of a round, pot-bellied toddler
Sparkles, and shines

Does not mirror the
Swirl of thoughts and emotions
Swimming through the adult's
Nostalgic, contented, excited eyes
Full of love and joy
For this little one's journey ahead

Youth on the path to knowledge
Processing information to gain wisdom
Living, aging, assessing and reassessing
Falling, failing, learning, triumphing
Finding certainty and sure footing

Soul searching and truth seeking
Until old facts dissipate, new truths surface
Playing in the shadowy mind regions
Growing greater gray areas
Vast black holes of the unknown

Noses pressed together
Gleeful toddler gaze locked
Onto grown-up eyes
Suspend worry, fear, challenges,
The pressing need to solve
The world's big puzzles

Life enjoyed day by day
Change guaranteed
Still sweet moments like this
Shall be savored forever

V.S. Chochezi

Mind speak

In conversation we speak
Quietly sometimes
Weak words of salutation
Commiseration lamentations
We squeak, squawk, and squall
Stalling inner voices calling
To be heard we gossip
Flap our jibs, beat our gums
Kick the can around, chop it up
Solve the problems of the world
We reason, negotiate, habla, hablo
Mitigate, litigate, commune
With spirits, lip sync song lyrics
Channel ancestors, karaoke
Okey dokey artichokey
Rolls glibly off the tongue
But those heartfelt words
Of how we truly feel
Get hung up in our mind's throat
And never see the light of day.

Staajabu

Old school

Yeah I'm an old head, got gray dread
Been around the block a few times
Get frequent senior discounts now
And don't have to stand in lines 'cause
The young folks step aside and offer
Me their seat – most times
Yes I'm a mature size
Got floaters in my eyes
High blood pressure, bursitis, plantar
Fasciitis and a little arthritis in my right hand
People tend to call me ma'am
When they take a mind to speak sometimes
Some call me auntie, sister, momma
Grand mom or old G though
There are days I feel twenty
Don't take planes or nothing fast
Like to walk on dirt or grass
Go to bed at nine get up at five
And give thanks each day that I'm alive
They say I'm way over the hill and
Yes I do take my pills, vitamins abcde
And damn near the whole alphabet, yet
I still tire just the same and my knees
Ache some when it rains
Though I'm not as well off as some
I'm a little better off than most
Still got some of my own teeth
Don't mean to boast but
I do keep up with the latest style
In my own way like what I'm
Wearing today for instance….
And as they say, ain't nothing shakin'
But the leaves in the trees and
They wouldn't be shakin' if
It wasn't for the breeze and
I'm the breezes blowin'
They call me old school.

Staajabu

Farm worker woman

Experienced hands
Smeared with fruit juice
She knows the earth and vines
She's visited treetops
Plucked apples from high branches
Picking strawberries
Picking grapes
She no longer smiles
No longer does she
Enjoy the sweet smells
And tastes

She works
She toils
The earth
She remembers

When she was
A small girl
She rose early
Picked berries
Ran up and down
Neat spacious rows and
She smiled often
The smells and tastes
Pleased her then
The sun hugged her each day
Crickets and other night bugs
Sang her to sleep each night

School she barely knew
And as she grew
The sun began to beat
Down on her
The rows closed in around her
Her world shrank
Pesticides poisoned her
Broken down houses
Were better than

Cardboard boxes
And filthy outhouses
Beat fly infested
Foul-smelling open
Holes in the ground
For a moment's relief

Dreams for her own
Children flowered
Then withered
She shivered
At night under
The naked sky

She never expressed anger
Only weariness
And now that she has
Learned the power
Of community organizing
She is mighty
Once again

She dreams
Of strawberry shortcake and
Blueberry pies
A sticky sweet smile
Plays on her lips
As she dips and drifts
Over groves and vineyards
Her future is brighter
Even if the coyotes not
The crickets and other
Night bugs now sing her to sleep

V.S. Chochezi

Jobs I've had

Jobs I've had have insulted my intelligence
assaulted my sensibilities
disregarded my humanness
ignored my culture
stifled my creativity
offended my morals
devalued my worth
sickened my spirit
diseased my body
disrespected my ancestors
underestimated my potential
and in some or many ways
contributed to the pollution
of this planet.

What about you?

Staajabu

Keepin' it real

Microphones become
Erogenous zones
While poets, singers
Rappers and emcees recount
Nearly endless
Fantasies of fantastic
Sexual exploits

But not a mention
Of latex escapes
Lips locked in reminiscent
Euphoric rapture

When erotica moments indeed lead to
Entwined bodies
Will thoughts turn to
Potential consequences?

Engaging in
Unprotected sex
Is like playing
Russian roulette

STDs, abortions
And HIV can be
Serious relationship killers
For real!

V.S. Chochezi

I live with HIV

Can't remember exactly when it
moved into my house, I think
it was in '82 when my friend
Humphrey's dance instructor
got sick with the disease and gradually
wasted away and Hump gave me
detail by detail of his demise I cried
with her many a day; then around '83
Al Delaney at Delaware State
told me about one of his friends.

Well Al was gay, crazy and always clowning around
and I thought he was joking
when he pointed his first two fingers
down and put his other index finger
across them to make an A
but he wasn't smiling not even a taste
HIV had come to stay

Because not long after that my sister-in-law
was infected by her husband,
then my oldest sister who moved to New York
with a bass player in Bill Doggett's band got positive
from using dirty needles and
my friend Ibeshe graduated from Berkeley
and one of her first jobs was at an AIDs clinic in West Oakland.
"Listen sistren, ANYONE can have aids" she said.
"You just don't know".

Then one of my cousins was diagnosed
and two of my nephews died of AIDS
and right after that my friend Phil
who graduated Columbia took a job
at Montefiore in New York
to direct an HIV program and he
tells me almost every time we talk, on the phone
in the most urgent tone "Look I'm telling you sis,
do not under any circumstance have unprotected sex.
Make sure you tell your daughter
and granddaughters that for me will you?"

Yes, I whisper, because it chokes me up to realize
how much he cares and how much suffering and pain
he has witnessed and because I live with HIV now every day.

No, I don't have AIDS but because of my family
and friends, their stories their sorrows,
their letters, their calls, their deaths –
HIV has come to my house to stay.

Staajabu

Where there was once ocean

Where there was once desert
There was once ocean

Where there was once ocean
There is now forest
Where there was once flatland
There is now mountain

Fault lines/earthquakes
Lava bed/volcanic eruptions
Hurricanes/tornadoes
Droughts and floods

The earth is ever changing evidently

Where there was once moisture
There is now fire
Where there was once heat
There is now ice

Where once there was wilderness
Now there is civilization
Where once there was peace
Now there is war

Technology advances
Life spans lengthen
Tempers shorten
Violence escalates
Poverty spreads
Life evolves

And somewhere in the
World today, another revolutionary
Is born

The earth is ever changing evidently.

V.S. Chochezi

Now what?

Made it
Completed it
Succeeded
Sensational

Wowed them
They loved it
Exhilarating

What next?

Top that
Sustain it
Do it again
Maintain it

Be outdone
Be washed up
Be yesterday's news
Risk boredom

Experience letdown
Anti-climatic end
Over it

Lost
Without purpose
Confused
Returned to normalcy
Got the humdrum doldrums

Oh yeah… it was spectacular!
Adrenaline junky?
Now what?

V.S. Chochezi

One shoe

There it was again one shoe, one shoe
laying in the middle of the street
What could it mean?
Was it an omen for me?
A premonition of my loneliness?
A commonness a hanging thought?
Incomplete and all like one shoe, one shoe
Laying in the middle of the street
Will you meet me, aw baby can you
Meet me down by the pylons?
Van Morrison asks and it always reminds
Me of one shoe, one shoe
Laying in the middle of the freeway
Causing all other thought to cease
Except the big question
I say the big question is
Whatever happened to the other, the
Others, the hundreds, thousands of
Mates that escaped the fate of homelessness?
Are they somewhere jamming with all the
Lost sunglasses, bic lighters and ballpoint
Pens laughing as their unfortunate partner,
Owner, possessor looks for them?
One shoe, one shoe, one shoe
Laying in the middle of the sidewalk
Why always in the middle?
Is that an omen too?
One shoe, one shoe, one shoe
Laying in the middle of the road and am I
Destined to be a lonely middle of the road
No name high top like the ones I see constantly
Mocking me while I look for the mate?
There must be a mate because everywhere you look
There are two of everything and one of me
And one shoe, one shoe, one shoe
Laying in the middle of the parking lot
Turned on its side another omen
Another premonition that all
My pent up hostilities will come out sideways

And one shoe will be thrown away in anger
And frustration like so many others
Making their way through a bedroom car truck window
Screen door narrowly missing a wife, husband
A belligerent youth, flying through the air
One shoe, one shoe, one shoe after another
Coming at me making me duck, take cover
Hug the nearest wall then turn to see it gazing at me
Tongue hanging out all large and long
In the middle of the space that used to be
My courage and the black inside
Beckoning to the space
That used to be
My mind

Staajabu

By the numbers

In the beginning cells divided and multiplied
and a species became by the numbers
we by the numbers educate our prescribed
number of children teaching them the
importance of numbers as soon as they can
say two-years-old then turn them over to
a school system that disburses funds
by headcounts and tax bases not faces,
not races, not places in need of more
because of poverty or language barriers

How many students in overcrowded
classrooms can sit and listen after
breakfasting on sugar/chocolate
marshmallow non foods while
watching cartoons that make them want to
run, shout, scream jump
hit somebody or tear something up?

How many can become creative, pursue
knowledge, invent, imagine, revolutionize
theorize, philosophize in this antiquated school
system where bore, bored and boring
have become the standard quip
spit from the lips of children
as young as five?

How do they survive teachers
whose sole purpose is to count heads then
count the ducats in their digit on pay day
whether they teach anyone anything or not?

By the numbers we declare a person educated
when they have studied a number of years,
completed a number of courses, written a number
of publications, and display a number of letters
after their name not by evaluating their intelligence

By the numbers students pursue careers instead
of vocations, callings, truths, passions or beliefs
seeking the highest pay with the least sweat
mustn't sweat, that is a big no-no in this
no sweat man, no sweat boss, no sweat
society where sweating is only allowed
in fitness centers

By the numbers we are losing our young
to consumer oriented happy happy happy
buy buy buy advertising which will teach them
the number of things to possess if
they want to be considered a success
regardless of the consequence, regardless
of the price, the highest being not a number,
but their soul.

Staajabu

Hunger

Perhaps elsewhere also
But overtly apparent In America
Most bellies are never empty
Most brains are primarily preoccupied

While most minds and spirits are
Mostly malnourished
Practically never content
Ever seeking, craving, hungering

Needing to be fed
Love starved
Needing to be satisfied
Needing to be fulfilled

Love sick
Needing to be healed
Needing to be held
Attention deficient

Wailing heart
Soul deprived

Perhaps elsewhere too

V.S. Chochezi

Patchouli anyone?

The patchouli
Brings warm greetings of
What's that you're wearing?
Where are you from?
Ummmmmmmmmmm,
Reminds me of something

Smiles, good vibes
Guidance and patchouli

Visiting lines in Vacaville
Trenton State
Standing at stop signs

What are you wearing?
That fragrance
What is it?

Are you from Africa?
How do you get your hair like that?
Are you a vegetarian?

My response almost always is

Patchouli....

And you?

Staajabu

Another day

Here I stand again
Caffeine racing through my veins
From the coffee I just drank
Rank and file working woman
Waiting at the copy machine
Caffeine urging me to jump hurdles
Run laps
Fingers tapping to the rhythm
While the machine mysteriously and ominously
Duplicates, and staples pages of facts and stats
By the hundreds with a green strobe light
And a clack tap squeak swoosh swoosh tap tap

Will a machine someday make copies of us
With a clack tap squeak swoosh swoosh tap tap?
Poems songs and rhymes come to mind
While keeping time to the clack tap squeak
Swoosh swoosh tap tap
Another day clack tap
Another day away squeak
From the things I love
Swoosh swoosh
Waiting
Tap tap tap tap tap tap tap
To go home.

Staajabu

The long haul

They tried to make sure we
Would never keep pace with him
Bound our feet in high-heeled
Pointed toe shoes
Shortened our stride with
Tight skirts, shirts and dresses
Impeded our education by
Making us feel less than capable
Said math, science, engineering
And medicine were out of our reach
Decreed marriage and babies
Best for weak simple minds like ours

They told us we could teach, type or sew
Anything but go where he would go
Walking fast in sturdy flat wide shoes
That fit his feet
Free to run, clothes loose and comfortable
Except for a tie or tuxedo sometimes
No household duties for him to detract
From inventing ways to keep us in bondage

They kept us ignorant of our moon cycle
Natural rhythm spiritual essence
Shaped this world just for him
To run free and keep us always
Trying to catch up while
Walking on our toes
Stuffing the pain somewhere
In the furrow of our brow
Considering one shampoo after another
Striving to become the long-necked
White rain head and shoulders ad
That makes eyes glow and grow
Warm with desire

Never wanting us to keep up but
Unable to keep us down
We've grown older bolder wise

Imagining his size twelve's jammed
To overflowing in size eight pointed toe
Black patent leather pumps
Running and stumbling
Feet blistering and bleeding
From an enormous effort
To keep pace with us
We study, plan and
Un-quietly wait

Staajabu

Don't hate

Fools be hatin on ya
Waitin on ya
To make a mistake

They just be hatin on ya
Waitin on ya to fall on your face

Can't stand to see you smiling
They want to see you cry

They just hatin, and debatin and
Telling each other lies

Somehow when you're standin tall
It makes them feel small

They think that when your light
Is shining they can't be seen
So they hatin on ya
Actin foul and treatin ya mean

You're good at most things
And even great at a few
You have talent, love, morals
Values and people who love you

And you're puzzled why these
Fools are out there breakin they necks
Just hatin on ya, waitin on ya,
Lackin respect

And all your time and effort
Go unappreciated
So now you're doubting yourself
And your confidence is shaken

And you know that the mistakes
Will come and you're certain
To fall from time to time

And they'll be standin on the sidelines
Laughing and enjoying your pain
Pourin cold water on you
While you're standin out in the rain

And now you're scared to make an effort
Afraid to improve
Cause the haters don't like it
And they be actin all rude

They say you're too smart
And you think you're so cute
And they callin you square
And sayin you ain't cool

So you avoid success
You slackin like them
But in this scenario,
Hey nobody wins

Let's rise above the haters
And do our very best
Let's try to jump the hurdles
And pass every test

Cause when they hatin like that
Know that you're on the right
Track and keep doing
Your thing as a matter of fact

Help them fools
Realize that the problem
Aint you
And that there's room
And opportunity
For them to succeed too.

V.S. Chochezi

Woman's work

Today right now, a young woman
Somewhere in the Sahara, Mojave, Gobi
Or Kalahari, China, Haiti, Africa, South America,
Mississippi, Appalachia, Mexico, Russia,
Greenland, Mongolia, Afghanistan, Australia
Is carrying a bucket, pail, goatskin, or
Pan full of water to her family
That weighs as much as she does
She walks a well worn path
Made by the many feet of the
Women who walked before her

There is a woman somewhere in the world
Right now collecting sticks, cutting down
Banana leafs, chopping down a tree,
Chipping a block of ice, making mud bricks,
Mixing clay with cow dung,
Raising pieces of corrugated tin,
A blanket or cardboard to make a shelter
As did the hands of many women before her

A woman somewhere in this world right now
Is being beaten by her father, husband,
Brother, a prison guard, maybe even her son
With nowhere to run for help or protection
And she has witnessed the same happen
To many women before her

There are women begging, rummaging,
Through garbage, stripping, borrowing,
Prostituting themselves, working two jobs while
Taking classes, driving with no license or insurance
Hiding from, police, bill collectors, and exes,
Eating less so their children
Will have more as they've learned
To do from the women before them.

As we sit and chit chat among ourselves
Tsk tsk, and shrug, suck our teeth and

Purse our lips indignant about the gangs and ho's
Street potholes, being left on hold,
Put on the back burner, a bus that doesn't show

While we complain about a program's late start
Long checkout lines at the supermarket
Freeway traffic, drug addicts,
Lack of art in the schools
There are young women in this world
Right now who will never see the inside
Of a classroom, know the freedom to choose
Their own mate, use a washing machine or
Refrigerator, go out on a date
As none of the women in their family, village,
Camp, compound, project or settlement have
Done any of these things before her

Whenever you pray, chant, turn inward and
Connect to the Most High Creative Energy in the Universe
Think of these women; send them positive vibrations
During your meditations as they struggle
With arranged marriages, genital mutilation,
Incarceration, war, famine, drought, floods,
Monsoons, hurricanes, earthquakes, disease,
Rape and loss that the load they carry
One day soon may be lighter and their path
Brighter and easier to travel
Than the women that came before them and

Remember we are being watched by
Young women all around us
They are not only learning from what we say,
They are observing everything we do and
Will follow the paths made by our many feet.
Let us do everything we can to insure
That the path we walk is a path of peace, power,
And positivity that will make life better
For the many women who follow after us.

Ashe

Staajabu

Chapter 2

Viewpoints

Maoni

Puntos de Vista

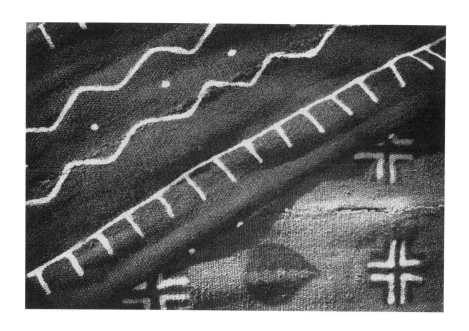

Resist

Resistance is not an easy road
Many have fallen from this path
Living a simple life's not simple
When there are so many things to have

Resist the lure of corporate greed
Resist buying more than you need
Resist the urge to hoard more and more
Resist the upscale department store
Resist the big cars resist the wars
Resist the seductive candy bars
Resist the fashions resist the shoes
Resist the chemically treated foods
Resist the brainwash resist the tube
Resist the government sponsored news
Resist the products that harm the earth
Resist the urge to splurge and splurge

Value facts value truth
Set an example for our youth
Help those less fortunate than you and
RESIST!

Staajabu

Next best revolutionary

Not all revolutionaries
Wear big afros, sport locs
Or shout, "I'm a revolutionary!"

Not all revolutionaries are born
With a permanent scowl
Not all revolutionaries
Are splashed on the evening news
And across the front page of the paper

Not all revolutionaries
End up in jail or
Shot up by the police
Or exiled to Cuba
Or Tanzania or
Participate in regular
High-speed chases

Not all revolutionaries
Wear red black and green
Or Malcom X shirts
Or Cesar Chavez shirts
Or Che Guevara shirts
Hats, pins or pendants

In fact, most revolutionaries
Sit in churches, not the
Infamous chicken establishment
But places of worship, churches
Mosques, temples, they teach in
Classrooms, they are clerks
In offices, they clean restrooms
They work on computers

They may sit quietly and meditate
They might not belong to
Any progressive organizations
They might fervently deny
Any revolutionary thought or ties

But if you look at any revolution
You will find that the masses make revolution

Individual, glamorized, villainized
Heroized historical figures have become
The face of revolutions but
They did not make revolutions
Alone

M.L. King Jr., Malcolm X
The Black Panther Party, Marcus Garvey
Rosa Parks, John Africa, Mao, Castro
Kwame Nkrumah, Gandhi, Mandela
Those are the names and faces we remember
But go back and look at the footage
You'll see scores and throngs
Of people who stood with them
But we don't know their names

Revolution is change
It usually seems sudden and drastic
And you may find yourself
Yes, your ordinary, everyday self
Caught up in the throes
Who knows?
You might even toss a stone
In the name of justice or
In protest of injustice

You might wake up, fed up
You could go to bed Joe Schmo
And wake up an instant revolutionary
No application necessary

Want to know what makes a revolutionary?
Want to know what one looks like in the making?
Go home tonight and take a hard look in the mirror
The next best revolutionary
Could just be you

V.S. Chochezi

Run

When they come at you with the GMO's
Run
When they try to sell you panty hose
Run
When the TV comes on by itself
Run
When you see sodas and soft drinks on every shelf
Run
When they make you an offer too good to be true
Run
When they suggest you'll look better in high heeled shoes
Run
When you read about the chemicals in your food
Run
Don't argue, reason or debate
Regardless of how much sense you make
They will make a zombie out of you
Faster than you can count to two so
RUNNNNNNNNNN!

Staajabu

How do you expect me

How do you expect me
Lil ol' me
To care about
What's going on in
Egypt or Tunisia, Zimbabwe
Or Rwanda
When my feet hurt
I have a headache
A backache, a toothache
And no Medicaid
No healthcare
I'm overworked and underpaid
And I don't even have a job
Seriously

How do you expect me
Lil ol' me
To overstand or even care
About MOVE or Mumia
Assata or Leonard Peltier
When my car broke down
It's two days after Valentine's
And I'm still trying to get out
The doghouse cause my significant
Didn't like my gift

Plus the price of gas is
Driving me insane
And there's only 300
More days left til Xmas!
Right.

How can you expect me
Lil ol' me
To worry about
Elections and politricks
Racism, sexism and classism
When my children
Are skipping school

My medical marijuana contact
Just moved
And they're talking about cancelling
The Real Housewives of Atlanta

Plus there may not be a football
Season next year if they
Can't come to terms of agreement
Now.

How in the world
Do you expect me
Lil ol' me
To overstand or even care
About the ins and outs of
Iraq, the war in Afghanistan
Issues between Palestine and Israel
U.S. police brutality
The criminal injustice system
Or preservatives in my food
When there are no nutrients in my food

And I lost my house to foreclosure
And I can barely afford my Starbucks jones
And they are shooting folks in
The barbershop on campuses
At the mall and the grocery store
And I don't feel safe anywhere anymore

And how can we expect anything to improve
If we… lil ol' we
Don't overstand or care enough to act
And work for change

V. S. Chochezi

Power to the people

They tryin' to run a game on us
We know it ain't right
Always talkin' 'bout some war
They want us to fight
While our air is polluted
The water is bad
And we got more chemicals
In our food than we ever had
They talkin' new-speak
Forked tongue politics
To keep us distracted and off balance
With their dirty tricks FCC, DOD, DOE
The big money people takin' over control
TV & newspapers selling their soul for
Money, machines and don't forget oil
Causing blood to spill on many a nation's soil
Every day you see where someone got caught
Lying, spyin', stealing, cheating or someone got bought
They got a scandal over here a scandal over there
Here a scandal there a scandal
Everywhere a scandal scandal
Enron here, Dubai there, here a Katrina,
There a BP everywhere a scandal scandal
Walmart here, Wall Street there,
FDA, CIA, NSA, NRA,
Everywhere a scandal scandal

Throw your fist in the air
And pump it like you really do care
And if you're tired of corruption
And you wanna do something everybody
Say oh yeah, oh yeah, oh yeah
If you believe in justice and you believe in peace
Everybody say oh yeah
Oh yeah
Oh yeah
Oh yeah

Staajabu

Governments play war games

Male dominated
Governments play war games
While civilians suffer

Starvation from sanctions
Wrack nations

Innocent people
Women and children
Cry, die
And wonder why
They are attacked
Bombings, fire, gunfire
Terror and death reign
When government
War games are played

Governments represent
People and Ollie North
Represented America
We joked about it
Remember? Probably not
And he and Reagan proved
That forgetfulness is a valid
Excuse for use in the courts

Tax dollars
Fund bombings in Iran
Kuwait, Panama and Vieques
But why should they hate us?

As they live in poverty
With death and disease
Poor water and electricity
Why hate America
And all its greed?

Innocent women breed
Governments, police, SWAT teams

Fighter pilots, armies
Navies, soldiers who then
Search and destroy
Loot and pillage
Rape and kill
In the name
Of national security

While we play
At Disney World
Watch soap operas
Sing and dance
Spectate our sports
And immerse ourselves
In entertainment

Governments play expensive
War games at our expense

They flex and threaten
They advance and retaliate
They kill and kill and kill
And wait

Governments are not
Mysterious entities
Void of names and faces
Without mothers and fathers
From different
Backgrounds and races

Governments are made
Up of people
And they represent us
Remember?

We must.

V.S. Chochezi

Recaptured splendor

After security checks
Emptying beverages
Baggage issues
High priced everything
Hurry up and wait, long lines
Aggravation and discomfort
Dampening the spirit and
Discouraging air travel

Finally seated
Cramped quarters
Ear-popping anxiety
Gum at the ready
Safety instructions completed

The engine hummed
Buzzed then roared
As the aircraft sped
Alongside the thick
Solid white line guiding
Us down the runway

Then quickly the nose rose
The plane inclined
And just like that
We were air-bound

Gazing down
Upon the city
Bright lights
Sparkled like a mound
Of gold and silver
Discovered treasure
And even at 10 pm
The horizon
Appeared lined with
Copper as if sunset
Lingered still

Awestruck!
Flying is still a marvel
The spectacle
Spectacular even
After all that was
Endured to
Experience it

For a brief moment
The splendor
Of those early days of
Flying was recaptured

The enjoyment of seeing
The world from the
Point of view of
The winged creatures
Both real and mythical
Is fantastic and simply splendid

V.S. Chochezi

Battles to be fought

Mankind's thirst for war
Seems endless
Battles to be fought
Battles to be won
Battles on the football field
Battles with real guns
Battles on the tennis court
Battles in the law courts
Battles on the golf course
Battles playing billiards
Battles playing cards
Some battles are won easy
Some battles are won hard
Battles on the big screen
Some even win awards
Battles in the conference room
Offense, defense strategies
Competition, struggle, rivalries
To be the best to be the lead
Fuels the present war machine
Battles on the television
Drug wars, bank heists
Gang wars, street fights
Battles to be fought
Battles to be won
Battles on computer games
Battles with real guns
Mankind's thirst for war
Seems endless from the
Cradle to the grave
So many ways to take a life
So few ways to save a life from
Battles to be fought.

Staajabu

The message

When slaves were granted freedom
With no money and nowhere to go
What message could be clearer?
When black people were refused
Education, jobs, housing, medication or
A ride on public transportation
What message could be clearer?
With the shameful treatment after Katrina
Of the black and poor in New Orleans
What message could be clearer?
With the high black unemployment and
Infant mortality rates, the number of deaths
Of innocent people at the hands of police
When they cut back welfare, dismantle affirmative
Action, cut food stamps and deny us reparations
What message could be clearer?
When they bombed the Philadelphia MOVE
Family killed 6 adults, 5 children
And burned down 61 homes on Osage
What message could be clearer?
When black neighborhoods are flooded
With drugs and guns causing self-destruction
Followed by amazing upscale gentrification
What message could be clearer?
Rosewood Florida, Birmingham Alabama,
Greenwood Oklahoma
Did you get the message?
Strange Fruit, Medgar Evers, Emmet Till,
Bobby Hutton, Paul Robeson, Fred Hampton,
Marcus Garvey, Dr. Martin Luther King, Amadou Diallo
Do you get the message?
The death penalty is legal lynching
Racism is still prevalent and unflinching
We must be diligent, be strong, be brave
For our children and grandchildren
We got a planet to save
What message could be clearer?

Staajabu

They should

They love euphemisms
Like discovered
When they really mean stole

They should celebrate
Columbus day
After all he paved the way
Over the lives of the Native people
Graciously and generously giving their land
This land to his own
The spoils of war no doubt

They should celebrate
Columbus day
But why should I?

They love euphemisms like
With justice and liberty for all
When they really mean
For all who can afford
To buy it

They should celebrate
4th of July
When America gained
Its independence
It's a historical moment
But as a slave descendent
Why should I?

They love to excuse their
Behavior with justifications like
That was in the past
I didn't kill any Injuns
And I didn't enslave anyone
But they will
Fly the flag high and
Sing the songs loud and
Proudly recall and reenact

Independence day and 1492
And look at you
Like you've got the problem
When you don't get all
Excited with them

And they will preach forgiveness
And encourage you to let it go but
They are still mad at you for being
Black and having nappy hair and
Living in their neighborhoods
And competing for their jobs
And going to their schools
And marrying into their families
And still being all black
And nappy and having the nerve
To expect equal wages for equal work

And got you doing everything
To try to be not so black and nappy
So you don't feel so unaccepted, inadequate
Inept, disrespected and disregarded

They.
They who celebrate
Columbus day and
Independence day
And hate on MLK Day and
Try to ignore Black History Month
The way I try to ignore Halloween
They.

They should
Let it go.
When they do,
I will.

V.S. Chochezi

Back of the bus

I sit in the back of the bus by choice
Reason one – The front is for the old and infirm
Reasons two, three and four – I want to see who gets on the bus,
Where they sit and what they do
Reason five – The back bus windows offer a panoramic view
Of Philly as it meanders down Walnut Street past
The dollar stores, delis and street vendors around 13th
The art stores around 21st the upscale
Boutiques and restaurants near 25th with the name
So small it could be the building's cornerstone
But for the box and bag carrying delicately heeled, layered in
Lace and leather, cashmere scarves floating
In the breeze customers easing in and out oblivious to the
Screeches, hisses, horn blasts and sirens
Surrounding them
Obviously insulated by money
They appear to be in an alternate universe
Untouchable, aloof, vision fixed on their next purchase
Or the chauffer who will pluck them from the carnage
And deliver them to their spa/yoga/brunch appointment
The windows give a clear view of the changing
Of the guard, don't even have to look to know that
Most of the color has disembarked and as the bus
Approaches the university district, nearing my
Stop near 35th
My thoughts remain with
The privileged people around 25th and Walnut wondering
What it must be like to ease in and out of upscale shops
Layered in lace, leather and delicate heels
Multicolored scarves floating in the breeze
Insulated and oblivious.

Staajabu

Excuse me?!

Double neck pop back
Hand on hip dip
Elbow raise, wave
Snap left, snap right
Eyes roll
Lips purse
Excuse me?!

Two words
Much attitude
A universe
Of indignation

Can I get some hot sauce
With that?

This democrat or
That republican corrupt politician
For office?

Invisible at the upscale
Department store counter
Or the common super store
Customer service checkout stand
Short changed at the fast food
Drive-thru
Or worse yet, they leave out
Some of the order

Damn! Where's my fries?
Excuse me?!

They keep claiming that
Reparations is going to
Bankrupt America
But just like that, they
Can come up with
150 billion dollars
To smack down Sadam

Chase around Osama
Search high and low for
Elusive weapons of
Mass destruction

Kill more people of color
In their own country
And wage the terrorism of war
Doublespeak for wage war
On terrorism

Please.

Double neck pop back
Hand on hip dip
Elbow raise, wave
Snap left, snap right
Eyes roll
Lips purse

Excuse me?!

When things just
Don't add up
When things
Just are not correct

When something is
Clearly amiss

Two little words
Much attitude
A world full of indignation

V.S. Chochezi

How do they oppress us?

Let us count the ways
They oppress us with every
Chocolate sugar-sweetened
Box of breakfast cereal
In colorful packages that
Seduce our youth and make them
Sugar addicts before they are two
They oppress us with twos in many forms
Two parties one aim,
Two choices evil and eviler
Two for one sales of merchandise we don't need

Let us count the ways we love our oppression
Oooooooh! DuPont we love your nylon
Trappings itching our legs while they run
They run and snag and we run to the
Nearest oppressor super store to grab
A new pair and what about the hairstyles
That oppress us more and more
Perms dyes straighteners extensions galore
Damage compliments of chemical companies
That are overjoyed to sell us a conditioner and
Repair kit after they have helped us kill
The hair follicle and we lose it
In the front and back after being
Attacked by the commercialization of the
Skewed perception of beauty that says
Your hair must be black, blonde, red, gold
Or platinum and sway in the wind
If you want to win or keep her or him

We can run but we can't hide
From the oppressor's ads that make us
Want to wear and chew
Whatever they want us to
Oh how oppressed we are and oh
How we love this abuse
We are the last to know we have been played
We are not playing radios TVs videos and CDs

They are playing us and oh how we love them
Especially our cell phones
So we NEVER have to be alone to think
That is the last thing they want us to do
They can't oppress us if we think for ourselves

Let us count the ways we can escape this oppression
Let us think of ways we can resist this oppression
Let us organize mobilize
Reclaim ourselves, be ourselves
Respect ourselves, love ourselves
Let us find a way
To break the chains of this oppression
So we can be really truly free.

Staajabu

Pieces lost

Look, I want my pieces back 'cause
I need 'em now that I'm getting old
I could do something bold with all those
Pieces of me that got cut away, pulled off
Combed out, broke off, the finger and toe nail
Clippings my mom made me flush
'Less some voodoo woman use 'em to
Work some roots on me hushed me as
She pulled clumps of hair out with that
Small tooth comb trying to tame my nappy
And make me look like Shirley Temple
Each torture session ending
With the stench of my pulled out hair burning
In an ash tray so the birds wouldn't
Build a nest with it and give me headaches
The rest of my life

I could be so much bigger, larger, fuller
Stronger, more confident and really
Full of myself if I had all of myself
All those pieces lost, tossed, flushed and burned
And where the hell are all the pieces
Of my pride, self esteem and self respect
That got shattered and splattered
When I was raped terrified, abused
Lied to and accused by people who said they cared
And can somebody tell me where my faith, hope
And charity have gone?
I need all the lost pieces
Of my heart to make me strong enough
To deal with all the mess going on
Like the Gulf oil disaster the financial melt down
Disaster, the bombing of the MOVE family disaster
The death penalty, Mumia Abu-Jamal
Leonard Peltier political prisoners and
Global warming and Traayvon Martin disasters

Where are all the pieces of my mind that
Went this way and that and got lost

Once or twice and somehow never
Really quite made it back where it belonged
I want the hair from under my arms
I had to keep shaved for years to look
Like a lady and skin off my chapped lips
The bunions cut off my toes want my
Teeth back that dentists pulled before
I learned to brush my teeth right I want
The tears I cried over everything
I want the sleep from out my eyes and the
Wax from my ears gone who knows where
I want all the cells, cuticles, itsy bitsy teensy weensy
Pieces of me back here right now
To make me big enough and fierce enough to
Take on this crazy rotten system.

Staajabu

An eye for an eye

What is she looking for in my eyes?
The supervisor who brings me work
Trying to look all in my eyes
What is she looking for?
My lids lower automatically
Shielding me from her piercing probing gaze
Do you understand she asks?
Yes I say looking at the work

What are you looking for in my eyes?
I want to ask each new oppressor
Who brings me work, brings me
Senseless jobs, assignments, tasks,
Projects and speaks in we's
We need to do this or that
When all the time they mean me
While bending their head sideways
Trying to look into my eyes

I wonder as I protect my soul from
Their prying gaze if they are trying to
Gauge my compliance, rebelliousness, my
Competence, disdain, or intelligence
Or are they searching for the secret of my survival
How I manage to work for so little pay and still
Take care of my family one day if they look too long
And hard I may have to quietly inform them that
If I should look back into their eyes,
As they are gazing into mine they
Would be risking their own demise
For the history of my people beats
Boldly in my chest my ancestors' words
Ring loudly in my ears giving me the power
To seize minds bend them to my will
And back people up off me without saying a word
I'm a revolutionary
Do YOU understand?

Staajabu

Undying faith

We knew we had to be careful of police
Protecting everyone and
Everything from us even in our neighborhoods

But we forgot about neighborhood watch
Watchin' us like it's their neighborhood
And we don't belong in it even though
We bought the house next door
It's not like we ran up on their porch and
Torched an ankh on their lawn
But when they got the guns and the laws and
The courts and the juries
And the judges and they own the
Airwaves and the papers
And the stores and the shops
And banks and the airports
And they control the jobs
And the jails
And basically the neighborhood
And the state and the country

And they socialize with each other
And think like each other
And empathize with each other
And they GET each other
And they acquit each other

And they fit right in
And you stand out like
A criminal with thief
Tattooed across your forehead

And you neglect to bow your head
Avert your eyes
Round your shoulders a little
And speak in soft tones of submission

Rather you react in indignation
Believing in your rights

MUD CLOTH ROOTS

In fairness and justice
Just to be reminded that
Everyone is not righteous

And they fail to recognize
Your humanity or demonstrate their own
And they wrench out your heart
And tear away your soul

And you end up with a situation
Like MOVE, Mumia, Leonard Peltier
Like Troy Davis, Trayvon Martin,
And Oscar Grant; like Amadou Diallo,
Abner Louima, James Byrd, Jr., Assata
And countless others

And really this is not a poem
About being Black or Native
Or "alien" or poor in America or Mexico
But you might be Palestinian
Or Aboriginal in Australia
Or you might be a kidnapped
Nigerian girl, one of 250
Who remain unfound

You might be a sex-trafficked slave
A victim of homophobia
A Muslim in Burma
A Dalit "untouchable" in India
A Cuban under the triple blockade
A woman subjected to rape
Murder, illiteracy, violence
And poverty in many parts of the world

And They are the enforcers and oppressors

Now complete optimism, belief that
Such things happen to others,
Denial or blissful ignorance
May prevent worry

But for the rest of us
Only our undying faith
In a mighty God
Small victories and random
Acts of kindness from people
We never expected we would
Relate to helps save us
From hopelessness and despair

We pray for divergence
From this destructive
Path of barbaric violence
Greed, self-righteousness
And subjugation of others
We are witnessing

You've heard it before
But it bears repeating
We long for human rights
And justice in a world
That embraces peace and harmony
Love and respect for all people

V.S. Chochezi

Reparations illustration

Take this poem
Mash it up into a
Nice round ball

Take the paper ball and
Throw it against the wall
Again, and again and again
Until you are exhausted
Unfold the ball and
You now have an example
Of what happened to
Black people kidnapped from Africa
Made into something
Unlike our original selves
Going up against many obstacles
And insults over and over again
Then exhausted and worn
Distorted, damaged and diseased
Found ourselves though loosened
From the gnarly knot of slavery
Seething, simmering, suffering
And keenly aware that we
Were once whole, balanced and
Beautiful -- like this poem.

We say
Reparations NOW!

Staajabu

Chapter 3

Love

Upendo

Amor

Black man

Your heart is carved from
A substance of deepest hues
From midnight sky
You move through
Millenniums leaving
Mind sets in your comet trails
They are searching for you
In the streets Black man
They want you on suspicion
Because you fit the description
They don't know who
You are and what price
They are going to pay
For their ignorance one day

Black man, come close
So I can hold you in my
Peaceful arms for a few
Minute's rest
It is your essence
That presents itself to my aura
You are larger than
Measurable time Black man
You eclipse everything else in sight
You light the night with your third eye
Your magnificent historical intelligence
Can never be forgotten
Just listening to your breath
Is my humblest gift
And to close your eyes in my
Presence the greatest compliment
Black man

Staajabu

Love sphere

(For all the nonbelievers especially those who have given up on love)

You will find love here
Love is here, right here
Look for it

It is not at all hidden
It is pouring out through the spaces
Between the words
Blackening these clean white pages

You will find love here
See it?
Flying off the page in 3D
Feel me?

Love is here
Right before your eyes
Take your mind off the thighs
And all that lies between see
If you can't find love
Maybe it's not what
You tend to seek

Love is a tricky thing
It's colorless, tasteless, odorless,
Yet infiltrates and fills the air
You CAN feel it, thick like humidity
Frizzin' up your hair

Or hot like a Sacramento summer day
Makin' sweat rivulets down your back
Or sweet like the misty aroma
Of freshly peeled tangerines
Or hot apple pie smells
Floating on airwaves
From the kitchen
Through the whole house
Out cracked windows
And halfway down the block

Or musty like after lovemaking
Mixed with scented candles and incense
Or crisp and clean like
At the top of a mountain
Burning your lungs a little
In early morning sunlight
Or fresh and steamy
Like the air carried on breezes
Blowing off the ocean at sunset

Hear it carried on waves
Slapping against the shore or
Sound waves through saxophone runs
Piano riffs, soulful melodies
And the tracks and
Songs of my sole lover
Can you hear it?

There is love here no doubt
Sliding from the gap in my teeth
Straight to your temple so
Be careful 'cause love can lead you to
Places you were not prepared to go

Close your eyes, cover your ears
And hide your heart
I promise you there is love here
In every fiber of my being
It's open and inescapable
Be wary lest it overwhelm you

There is love here
Right here, where you will find it
If you dare
To bear witness
That love lives
In this love sphere.

V.S. Chochezi

Met her at low tide

Met her at low tide
Dipped a toe in
Found it pleasing
Went for a swim
Spent days walking along the shore
Collecting seashells and colorful rocks

Heard the storm forecasts
Ignored all the warnings
Never understood the full potential
Of the ocean
Didn't prepare, didn't even have a clue
The tsunami wreckage was great

When it was over
He talked a good game about
Going back to the beach
Wanting to surf and jet ski

Wrote poems about
His love for the sea
Reminisced about those good
Times spent with salt water
Sand and gorgeous views
Across the horizon

But finally understanding
That low tide wasn't the whole picture
That calm waters don't remain calm always
That the ocean's beauty could be deathly deceptive
His talk never turned to action
And they never laid eyes on each other again.

V.S. Chochezi

Clean love

We met on a bus became friends
then lovers moved in together
he hated his work had secrets
loved me from a far off land I could
feel in his thick heavy dread he led
I followed because his far off love
was more tender and sincere
than any of the possessive ego
involved mechanical obligatory
copulations of my past

We had no car and no washhouse near enough
to walk to so I washed our clothes by hand
and didn't mind because we both loved the
smell of wind and sun in our small place
that mingled with the frankincense and
wafting whiffs of cumin, fava beans, collard
greens, goat cheese, dolmas, coffee, along
with the nag champa, patchouli, marijuana
aromas on the clothes of visiting friends speaking
Arabic, Swahili, Spanish, French, Jamaican Patois
Louisiana Patois and Ebonics on weekends

Our pallet was full soft and clean
he slept still his body dark ebony, long
lean sinewy, face full bearded and peaceful
the last night we spent together

The call came from his friend in broken English
he was gone and my only solace was the comfort
of knowing that when he gently kissed my forehead
and left for work that morning
everything he wore even his coat had been
freshly washed and smelled of wind and sun

Staajabu

Swooning

Like a quiet morning
Broken only by birdsong
Soft wind rustling
Leaves in trees
Like predawn lullabies
Waking me out of sleep

Love makes joy
A bit more joyful
Happiness is happier
Good intentions become
Good deeds
Love poems are
Sweet on my ears
Love music moves me

Simple acts capture
My heart and my
Love's presence
Corrects my balance so
Good posture is better
Back straighter
Neck erect
Walk more upright
And purposeful

Like throngs of stars
In a clear night sky
Galaxies away yet
Almost within reach

Like sun warmth and
Soft rain love offerings fill
The heart with hope
For beautiful tomorrows

Love connection
So full of possibilities

Telephone kisses
Internet love notes
Cuddling all night
Thoughts of you
Loving me loving you
Make my day
Love makes my day
Thoughts of you love
Make my day so full
Soulful soul full of life

Could trip on this love
All day and night
After night
After timelessness

Trying to fit it in
This short poem looking
For the perfect ending
'Til reams of paper flow
Like rivers and still there'd
Be so much more to say

But before this gets
Completely carried away
Trust and believe
Love makes
Joy more joyful

V.S. Chochezi

Don't be fooled

Don't be fooled
By the words of
Young romance poets.

The truth is... drum roll
please...
Love STINKS.

Really.
You want more closeness
They pull away
You want more space
They grow clingy

You love them
They love you too
But not in the same way

You love them like
Bonnie and Clyde
Or Winnie and Nelson
Before he got out of prison
Like Angela and George
Or Ossie and Ruby Dee

They love you
Like a favorite cousin

Even when love works
As in you love them
And they love you more
A perfect union
It's all bad.

See love is full of
Vulnerability it
Opens you up to
The worst kind
Of betrayal

You must be
Infinitely forgiving
Or incredibly stupid
To love well for long

Talk about disappointment
And heartache!
Which am I?
I've been both
But today
Today I am neither

So when I tell you
I love you
Please overstand
That I don't believe
In love anymore
Still, it's a hard
Habit to break

Listen.
I'm just telling
The truth
Not trying to
Influence you for
Profit or gain

Love is a drug
Or at best a commodity
For the consumer machine
That is America.

Diamond rings, flowers
Greeting cards, and bakeries
Thrive on it
They want you to
Believe in love because
It lines their pockets

If you want to be
Free and happy
Let go of love
And avoid young
Romance poets
Idealistic, ignorant fools
Who don't know any better

Trust me.
Happiness is hormonal
Freedom is destiny
Love is a fantasy

And just like all
Society had you hyped
Up on Santa
They've got you
Psyched out on love

When you grow up
You perpetuate both lies
Because it's proper etiquette
Well, I'm letting the cat
Out the bag

The emperor HAS no clothes!

And care, concern, honesty
Respect, responsibility
And reliability are so
Much better than romance

Now don't be fooled
By the mouths of young
Starry-eyed romance poet

The truth is…
Love --- STINKS

V.S. Chochezi

Love that, that will love you back

I love my bed and my bed loves me
I love to be all snuggled and cozy
covered and secure
enjoying the nice slow relaxation
that pours over me
savoring the last few waking moments
before my bed and I become one and
drift together into the beautiful and
lovely, spiritually resuscitating
physically rejuvenating
state of marriage called sleep
where body and bed are wed blissfully
united throughout dream-filled hours
while forsaking all others

And without a doubt
my bed loves and supports me
which is why I am reluctant to leave
even when I need because I know
it will miss me until I come again weary
answering its call to recapture the feeling
my welcoming, wonderful bed gives me
I love my bed, I love my bed
and my bed loves… ZZzzzzzz

Staajabu

Love and romance

You say you want to hear love poems
You anticipate soft kisses on ears
on back of neck, down spine
locked eyes, bodies entwined
poems

And I drench your world with passion
charge the air with heat, and invite you
to join my rhythm

I'm talkin about love and romance

I make your heart beat wildly
for the love of truth, passion for justice
love of family, passion for righteousness
love of creativity, passion for the word
love of learning, passion for protest

I am full of love for life
but my romantic fantasies
have not found a way
through pen to meet page

Publicly to share romantic fantasies
my gift is not—yet, though sought

Seek not my tales of intimacy
for there you'll find
generations of heartache
acres of disappointment
leagues under deep seas
of broken, empty promises
gurgling alongside
mountains of beautifully
delivered, soulfully rendered
outpourings of false or
fleeting romantic
words like "I love you"

Which could result in
I'll be home
bitter and alone poems

Can you pay
your own bills poems

Can you tell
the truth sometimes poems

Can you pretend like
it's not ALL about you
for just one minute poems

If your children
see the sitter
their teachers and
their grandparents
more days in a week
than they see you
do you really think
you're raising them poems

Children need to eat everyday
and they need guidance
every day poems

Can you feel the love?

Can you feel the love?

Now I see in your eyes
that though you say
you want to hear love poems
a mother's devotion
to her children
a grown child caring
for elderly parents
Che Guevera putting
his very life on the line
for his people

Love, beautiful, complete
committed, divine
No, love is not what you had in mind

You say you want to hear love poems
you anticipate erotica, exotica,
roses, candles, diamonds
and cupid's arrows
ooh ah poems
nitty gritty doo wa ditty poems

I offer you passion
I pen it in rhyme
and lay it heavy on your mind

When you feel true love
will you recognize
appreciate and enjoy it?

Or will you overlook it
take it for granted
and destroy it?

You say you want to hear love poems
And I ask you
Can you feel the love?

V.S. Chochezi

Dancing in the junk

Daniel and Aiesha were lovers
Who worked the flea markets
She black and thin, hair askew
Jamaican accent mixed with
Islamic phrases and a
Ras Tafari or two
Sold incense

He Chicano, golden brown
Thick black hair mixed with gray
Army fatigue jacket worn
Like he meant it sold golden
Moldy oldies amidst stacks
Of used books and magazines
Piled almost to the ceiling
But leaving an aisle wide enough
For these lovers to dance

They danced the slow drag
And held each other close
Marvin Gaye's voice rose
To the rafters and though you
Could hear flea market laughter
The couple would stop often
To help a customer buy a CD
Egyptian musk and patchouli
And as soon as they walked
Away Daniel and Aiesha were
In each other's arms again
Cheek to cheek dancing
To Love on a Two Way Street
Like they were at the dance hall
On Saturday night
Instead of in the middle
Of a barn full of junk
At the Sunday flea market

Staajabu

Prisoner of love

When he picked me up from the Laundromat
he asked about the man I was talking with
at the folding table and the next day he bought
a washing machine

One day he saw me talking with the
next-door neighbor while hanging up clothes
in the back yard and the next day he bought
a clothes dryer

He saw me talking with people at the bus stop
so he started driving me to and from work and
when my parents called he listened in on the
extension phone, said it was too dangerous
for me to walk, run, bike or shop alone

I spoke of taking piano lessons from a
master pianist at a shop downtown
so he bought a beautiful piano in perfect tune
along with how to play books inside a blue
and brown tapestry covered piano bench

One night after dinner I washed the dishes
while he sat at the kitchen table reading the paper
when he went to the bathroom I retrieved my
coffee can stash, gathered the trash took it out back
walked quietly through the gate down the alley
to the main street boarded a bus slouched down in the seat
and contemplated my new freedom and solitude

Staajabu

About love

I love you
Like hands love fingers
Like feet love toes
Like lungs love air
Like heads love hair

A natural, perfect fit
We just belong together
Like PB & J
Our lives entwined and
You are always, always
On my mind

I'm anticipating your needs
Your wants, your every desire
I love you
I love you!

I ...Loved you
Like the ocean loves water
Like fire loves heat
Like healthy gums
Love strong white teeth

And now, somehow
A joint home has become
A single dwelling
Our children became
Joint custody

Our love has become
A distant, cloudy memory
And this is only partly my story
Some of it doesn't belong to me
So if it sounds familiar
It could be yours

See I've been in love
A time or two before and sometimes

I might seem confused but
To tell the truth
I know EVERYTHING
I need to know about LOVE

Love makes you feel stronger
Fortified, practically invincible
Love lifts you up and makes
You want to skip, dance, smile
Whistle, shout, sing and do
The right thing

Control, manipulation, jealousy
Envy, tit for tat and suspicion
Simply does not fit within
The definition

Of course you've got to take
The good with the bad and
The ups with the downs
But if you upset me, reject me
Abandon me

If I am too often alone, unhappy
Uncomfortable or in doubt
If my needs and wants go
Too long unmet
Then you best bet
I learned that I don't
Need to stop loving you
Unconditionally to leave

And all you have to do is
Look at me to see
But if the looks don't tell you
The words should
Help you believe
And if you have the time
Then watch my deeds

Because between all three
You'll find that

As much as I love you
I indeed love ME!

I love me like grass loves rain
Like flowers love bees
Like bears love honey
And skies love trees

If you love and runaway
You could live to love
Another day ☺

See love is not rude
Love doesn't batter
Love shouldn't bruise
Love is considerate
Love is pleasing
Love is passionate
Love is visible

So if you love me
I won't have to guess
I'll know
Your words will tell me
And even better
Your actions will show!
And we can live happily
In peace love and harmony
The true beauty that is
You and me in love

But this is only partly my story
Some of it doesn't belong to me
So if it sounds familiar
It could be yours

V.S. Chochezi

Chemical Reaction

Kwansaba (7 lines, 7 words per line, no word has more than 7 letters)

When my love walks into my view
Where I be just doin' my thang
My inner light emits bright spirit rays
Beams on all so they say wow!
What's with you all aglow in beauty?
Certain, secure, smile wider, wrapped in peace
When my love walks into my view

V.S. Chochezi

Giving thanks and praises

When I woke up this morning
I had love on my mind
A real strong feeling of love on my mind
I was feeling full to bursting with the most
Intense love of life love of family
Love was swelling up inside of me like a
Water balloon making me want to shower
This love on the world, a world I loved
This day with all its good, bad,
Beauty, flaws and imperfections

There was a grateful loving feeling for
The bus driver, the nice clean bus
The iPod-listening, texting, email checking
Kindle, paperback, newspaper
And magazine reading
Talking loud on their cell phone, staring
Into space, heads lolling and nodding
Passengers riding with me

I felt love for the beautiful country landscapes and
Busy colorful city scenes along the route to my office

And oh how I loved my job today
Because it provides me with money which
I love so much to have and which makes
My pleasant and peaceful life enriched
And enables me to share with others

I knew this day would be filled with love
Because when I woke up this morning
I had love on my mind and was giving thanks
And Praises to The Most High for love
In all its many and varied forms and for the
Realization that I am love, I am loved and
Love is visible, tangible, audible and very
Very real.

Staajabu

Chapter 4

Poetry and Words

Mashairi na Maneno

Poesia y Palabras

Joyful abandon

My life is lived
in short spurts
quick bursts
of joyful abandon

Between red ink
over black and blue
letters on white pages
write, edit
delete, rewrite

Be precise, concise
be clear; don't veer
from style guides

Correct grammar
Punctuation, spelling
Rules

Focus, concentrate
Don't err; don't fail
Don't deviate

'Til eyes tear
Words blur
Commas splice
Infinitives dangle

And prepositions
End sentence
After sentence
After sentence

Strike through
White out
Back space
Erase

But I can't give a damn
About typos anymore

Poor writing might pass
By a tired, burnt out
Lazy editor
Especially if
If it's mouthed over
A loud, catchy beat

But it won't be
Confused with
Won't pass for
Creative license

Even creating
A fresh poem
Dictates a certain
Measure of discipline

Create, practice
Rehearse, flow
SLAM

And it all returns
Sankofa
Go back and fetch it
Full circle
To poetry
Breath, Breathe
Life

My life
Is lived
In short spurts
Quick bursts
Of joyful abandon

V.S. Chochezi

Poetry is my thang

Maybe fifty years ago or so
It was okay to write poems about birds
Bees, flowers and trees but
These days nature has been perverted with
Additives, pesticides, pollution, fluoride
Hormone chicken, bees raised for honey
Trees grown for money
Landfills, oil spills, genetically
Modified foods… killing us softly
Poems are lame to me
If they don't speak change to me
I want to hear poems about
Creating a world where all
People will be able to live healthy
Fruitful lives fulfilled
I want to hear poems that speak of
Human rights, civil rights, women's rights
GLBT rights, worker's rights, prisoner's rights,
Senior's rights, children's rights, the right
To live without the threat of nuclear war
Or man-made diseases killing us softly
I want to hear truth talking' in-your-face poems
About the poor, unemployed, homeless
People in the world, corporations
Destroying our rainforests
Governments vowing to reach
And pollute another planet
While acting like they don't know
What's causing cancer on this one as they
Sell us products to eat drink drive smoke and wear
That are killing us so softly
You know poetry is my thang but
I only want to hear revolutionary poems
Speak to me of change y'all
Speak to me of change y'all
Or you will not speak to me at all

Staajabu

Blank page

A thought jumps in
Triumphantly headed
For the blank page
The writer rejoices

A knock on
The door interrupts
The right thing to do
Would be to
Ignore the intruder

But the civil, socially
Well-adjusted individual
Dutifully answers

Returning, religious
Pamphlet in hand
The writer heads back toward
The goal whistling happily

Nature calls and is addressed
Thought still intact, yet fading

The writer heads toward
The blank page again
The phone rings

The intelligent writer
Listens as the caller
Leaves a message
Call me back, it's important!

The rebellious writer
Sits at the computer
Email is open

Urgent message
Is the top line
The writer is sucked in

50 minutes later
The pamphlet is filed
The email is answered
The phone call is returned
The thought is gone
The page is blank.

V.S. Chochezi

Pain is

Pain is always with us as poets
We ache for love
Cry for peace and yearn
For the beautiful agony
Only we can feel

Pain is always on the brink
Of the poet's eyelash
Sobbing of our shortcomings
Tearful at words only we can hear
Keening for more of the lost moment
When we envisioned at light speed
The answer to everything

Fearful and terrified that our thoughts
Will vanish with the morning light
Dark is our friend
We see poems so clearly in the dark
Where the pain lurks waiting
To be told

Staajabu

Poets are going to poet

Audience or no
Welcome outlet
Or hostile environment
Poets are going to poet

You can turn your back
Cover your ears
Shout obscenities and heckle
You can banish and exile
Cut funding and pass laws
But poets are going
To express or implode
Forbid them to write
They will whisper
Outlaw whispering
They will drum
Destroy the drums
They will tap and hum
Block humming
They will dance
And crunk and paint
And tag and rap

Poets are going to
Express and like Maya's
And Still I Rise
Like Neruda's
Exile in Chile
The people
Will grab hold
Of the poem
It will take on
A life of its own
You will hear it
Wherever you go
Poetry is a product
Of the universe
It won't be stopped
Crushed or killed

See poets are strong willed
They inspire others
To reach within and
Poets birth poets
So there is always
A ready supply
And you can shout sit down
You can scream
Nobody wants to hear it
You can yell
Who cares?

They may stash
Their expressions
In drawers and mouth
Them quietly to
Themselves
They may poet in
Their sleep and
Sneak them into songs
But admit it or not
Poetry cannot be stopped

A tight-lipped
Tight fisted poet
Is on the verge
He may litter
Your email box
With a slew of words
She may hand you
A binder as thick
As an encyclopedia
Don't let a frustrated
Subjugated, muted poet
Corner you
Trust me because poets
Are going to poet!

V. S. Chochezi

Slam poets

Slam poets command words
With quiet strength
Walk gently, talk smooth
Slam poets lean forcefully into each phrase
With ease and confidence
Comfortable before a large crowd
Or an intimate few

They will share a view or two when asked
Mask set concentration unbroken
Private thoughts remain unspoken
Minds are sharp memories keen
A mic and audience is all they need
Food for them is praise and applause
And they will gladly perform for
A worthy cause

Off the cuff they can recite a sonnet
Or a half hour poem about planets and comets
Slam poets are still a question mark
They seldom reveal what is in their heart
They would have you think the poem is them
But their primary concern is that they win
Then take the prize in hand having been
Declared victor of the slam

Staajabu

Words

...Are powerful
Words can inspire
Motivate arouse
Create imagery
Paint pictures
Spark ideas
Words can last
Forever
In the beginning
There was the word
Words can float
Fly soar and sing
Words are mighty
Words can stick in your
throat, fall flat and die
Words can hurt, hit and
Hate; words can lie
Words can imitate, mock
Jeer, annoy, whine, shout
Scream, yell, denigrate and
Dismiss
Goodbye

Words can
Love, flirt
Seal the deal
I do. Ashe.

Words create bonds
Words forgive
Words offer
Second chances
Words live
Words are
Chameleons
Words can
Change texture
Tone and mood
Words are dangerous

Words exist
Words can be
There are plenty
Words and
When words
Don't work
We make up
New ones
Words are born

Words can hide
Mask, exaggerate
Embellish, deceive
Distract, destroy
Radiate negativity
Echo negativity
Stifle creativity
You'll never amount
To anything

You can't
It's impossible
Words can be
Empty
They can mean
Nothing
They can rot
And stink
They can be
Broken like
Unfulfilled promises
Words are potent
Words can fight and

Words can play
Words are magical
Words are poems
Words are useful

Words are seldom
Just words

Words can question
Like – what does it all mean?
What is the truth?
How many words exist in all
The languages on earth today?
What will you do with words?
What will you do with these words?
From where do words originate?
How do words come together?

Consider the source
Words are spiritual
Words are reflections
Words are energy
Words can bless or
Be blessed

And even with all that
Words are and can be
Words alone
Are not enough.

V.S. Chochezi

Tumbling inside out

Tumbling inside insides tumbling
frustration builds building frustrations
breathing constrictions constrict breathing
seeking relief through words
trapped in the depths of despair
loneliness and feelings of lowliness
helplessness, rumbling and tumbling,
turning insides into dammed up words as
rising tides of anger, frustration
unrequited love, need of affection
unanswered questions, unsolved
mysteries, unresolved issues,
pills being ineffective in treating
global warming, industrial pollution
nuclear threats, never-ending wars
discrimination, corruption and lies
looking for words

there must be words because
in the beginning there was the word
looking for words to describe then
prescribe a cure, a way out a word out
searching for outlets to let out, bleed out
breathe out, shell out, pour out and
shout out words
to quell the tumbling,
jumbling constrictions causing our
unspeakable pain that must be spoken
shared, declared, confessed, professed,
unleashed, released out loud with the
accompaniment of grunts groans sighs
cries screams and moans as others
witness and testify, testify and witness
our agonizing anguish and pain
so the healing of our mind/body/soul
in the midst of much fanfare, ranting
and raving can really truly begin.

Staajabu

Chapter 5

Cosmic Routes

Nija Cosmic

Rutas Cósmicas

Prayer for the planet

To the Most High Creative Energy
In the Universe that connects us all
And beyond

Oh Creator of all things great, small
Gigantic, colossal, microscopic, infinitesimal
Seen and unseen

Please guide us in our struggle on this small orb
That we may fulfill our creative destiny
Cast and chartered by your infinite wisdom

Protect us from senseless violent acts
Toward one another and may greed, apathy
Jealousy and hate be healed in all of us afflicted
And may we consciously consider the health
Welfare and beauty of our Mother Earth in
Everything we do, forever and ever and ever
A-woman
A-man.

Staajabu

Theoretically speaking

Since matter is neither
Created nor destroyed
And since in some
Sense we are matter...

We were neither
Created nor destroyed

Then some part of us
Has always existed
And will always exist

Just in some
Other form.

This concept combined
With imagination and
Creativity certainly can
Produce notions

Ranging from reincarnation
As a tree, a bird or
Another human being...

Or ascending into heaven
Plunging into hell
Mud to man
Dust to dust

Ahhh the possibilities
Are as endless as our ideas

And we, at the very least
Are in this way eternal.

V.S. Chochezi

Spirit voices

The spirits have spoken
Let your soul be redeemed

The axe has fallen
Let your works be seen

As the blade emerges
From authoritative lips
Statues, baskets, symbols, signs
Wood and metal bits

Human hands fashioned all
Human minds conceived them

Human dwellings housed them
And human hearts believed them

Breath, sweat, blood, sacrifice
And ritual invoked them

We received their messages
The spirits have spoken

Spirit voices carry
In the rhythm of the drums

You can feel the edict
When a chorus group hums

Their verdict
It is carried along on the wind

Their judgment is pronounced
Again and again

Their judgment is final
Though not so grim

The truth is evident
Babies cry it
Birds sing it
Silence screams it
Rain beats it

You have heard it
With your very own soul
Now the challenge
Is to accept it

The chorus echoes
Throughout the land
Hear it; heed it; overstand

Protect mother earth
Respect one another
Take good care of
Your father and mother

Give freely
Reject greed

Self-preservation and defense
Is the natural law creed

A shimmer of recognition
Glimmers in your eye

Inspired by the unifying voices
Material differences unhide

Cultural cohesiveness
A universal code

The spirits have spoken
Redeem your soul

V.S. Chochezi

Coming into over-standing

Searching for reasons
Rationale
A touchstone
Answers to questions
Lodged in hearts and minds
Floating in limbo where
Unseen tentacles of electrodes
Extend toward any sign any signal
Red light green light amber
Hanging on the corner
Waiting for the number
Waiting for the ship the slip the tip
That will take us to the
Tablet the tableau the dresser
The bureau the canister the
Banister the balance the chalice
The nectar the connector the
Meaning of our waking and sleeping
Walking and talking inhaling and exhaling
Crying and dying while the trees and
Galaxies observe objectively our
Never ending struggle to know

Why?

Staajabu

Forgotten Truths

Perhaps dead languages
Hold the truth of the history
We have forgotten

So lies can blossom as new
Truth, THE truth after all
What proof exists to
Refute interpretations
Of the past beyond
Our observations, deductions
Intuition, cell memory
Legends, stories, myths
Old wives tales and epic
Poems passed down
Through generations

V.S. Chochezi

Empowered

Truthfully,
His disrespect
Prompted her
To turn her back
On the world
Not shame or
Fear but deep disappointment
Had her antisocial

But it was God that called her inward
Focused on prayer meditation
Enlightenment and self-improvement
Emerging whole and empowered
Ready and steady to meet
Any harsh gaze

Go ahead
Disapproving
Eyes cannot pierce
The transparent heart
Higher love awaits
Healing happens
Transcendence

V.S. Chochezi

No loss to grieve

When you draw a bucket of water
From the river
Does the river miss it?

Perhaps. But its absence is not evident
No gap, no hole, no mark remains
To remind us that something is gone

The river never even pauses
Just flows along on its journey as always
Seamlessly connected
Yet easily separated

Could it be because it knows
The separation is truly an illusion?

Even as you carry the bucket away
Water droplets slide down the bucket sides
Slipping to the ground
Perhaps hydrating a tree

Perhaps evaporating into the air
Feeding a cloud, always preparing to
Rain back down into the waterways
Back to the river

Even as you drink it, it soon escapes you
And so it seems there is a greater connection
Among water that the river overstands

Never lamenting the loss of its parts
Always working to reunite and
Sometimes my love moves this way too

Connecting completely
Then separating
Though never looking back

Realizing that we are
Humanly composed of at least
70 percent water

I will not miss you when we part
For we share an eternal connection

There is no loss to grieve
Only memories to appreciate
And we will all reunite
One day at the same place…

At the source.

V.S. Chochezi

Upon further reflection

I know I said I will not
Miss you when you are gone
But upon further reflection
What I meant was
Of course I will miss you

When we part ways
It will not be a sad
Grieving mourning kind of
Missing you

Rather it will be
A nostalgic affair
Reveling in the
Good times we shared

Perhaps even romanticizing
The tense moments
The times of doubt, mistrust
And even betrayal

And the many instances of
Forgiveness and moving
Forward harmoniously
Yes, upon further reflection
Of course I will miss you

Not a terrible, panged
Longing to see you kind
Of missing you

But an occasional
Acknowledgement of
The soul experience
That contributed to
My development as
Part of life's journey.

V.S. Chochezi

Many paths

Although I do not
Claim Islam
My prayers often begin
And end with Bismillah
Allah Akbar

Although Christ is one
Of the world's greatest creations
Christianity cannot possess me
For God speaks to me
And through me, directly
And has taught me
That there are many
Paths to paradise

And whether standing or kneeling
Eyes closed or open wide to the sky
Hands clasped or outstretched
My prayers are received
Not rejected upon technicalities

And though I do not count myself
Among the Buddhists or the Hindus
Karma is an important part of my
Vocabulary and daily life

And while I find ital food irie
Love my hair nappy
Bump reggae music regularly
And praise Jah mightily
Rastafarian I am not, exactly

Admiring my sister Ifa priestesses
And my brothers entrenched in the
Yoruba traditions, erecting alters
To their Orishas
You will often find me
In their company

Soaking up their wisdom
Yet I have not been initiated

You may hear me
Thanking Amen Ra
See me wearing an ankh
Observe me reading the Husia
And catch me contemplating Ma'at

Keeping in mind that
Dr. Karenga is no saint
That Kwanzaa is not a religion
And that honoring our ancestors
Is not ancestor worship
I give much credence to the
Nguzo saba and live
By the principles of
Unity, self determination
Collective work and responsibility
Cooperative economics
Purpose, creativity and faith

Now, you might
Find me searching
And think me lost
Might seek to define
My beliefs in religion
Might challenge me to pick one
Choose one road and stick to it

Yet every turn shows me truth
Every day brings me light
Every stretch brings me insight
Every holy one leaves me
More whole
I gather what I can hold
And leave what does not
Empower me
And I have truly been blessed

Only time will tell
But when our paths cross

Know that I come in peace
And hope to leave in peace
Our lives more enriched
For the experience

My friends accept me
You may love me
Leave me
Hate me or reject me

But as Tupac said
Only God can judge me

V.S. Chochezi

Peace

If people ever realized the true value of peace
We would want peace instead of diamonds
Gold or one hundred dollar bills
If people ever really understood
How wonderful and rare peace was
It would be advertised in every medium
And everyone would have to have some

If people ever came to the realization
That everyone on earth has a right to
Live in peace and how wonderful that
Life could be if they had it
There would be tennis shoes named
After it dances called by it children
Named names like Peace Everlasting
And everyone would have to have some
If people ever connected with the idea
Of peace and the spirit of peace
There would be books, movies,
TV programs and conferences about it and
Everyone would be trying to get some
And the people with the most peace
Would be the most respected

If our so called leaders ever came to know
Peace themselves in their homes
In their lives they would not be doing all
The crazy things they are doing right now
And they would be trying to make sure
That everybody had some

If people only knew the value and rarity
Of peace they would greet each other with peace
They would offer each other peace
They would teach peace and show peace
In everything they did and even the
Children would ask for peace instead of candy

If people ever truly reached
A peaceful state of existence there would
Be peace dances every Friday
Peace rallies every Saturday
And peace sessions every Sunday
If every home knew peace
Every office knew peace
Every school knew peace
Every song sang peace
And every soul found peace
We would say peace instead of thank you
Peace instead of goodbye
Peace instead of I love you
We'd be full of harmony and happeeeeee…
And EVERYONE would have some. Peace!

Staajabu

Chapter 6

Natural Sense

Maana ya Asili

Santido Natural

If you could just hear

If you would just listen
If you would just listen

Mother earth is speaking
Her messages are clear
If you would just listen
If you could just hear

If you would just listen
She's sending a warning
With global warming
Rain, floods, drought
Signs of pain
Tsunamis, tornadoes
Blizzards and hurricanes

She's begging
She's pleading
Stop the madness
Stop the insanity
Stop the wars
And destruction
Cease the vanity
Save humanity

If you would just listen
If you could just hear
Her messages are clear

Cease killing for oil
Stop destroying the soil
Underground nuclear testing
Satellites in space
Disrupting the earth's natural
Balance and pace

If you would just listen
If you could just hear
The ancestors are near

They are trying hard
To get through to you
If you would just
LISTEN

They're shouting
They're whispering
In bird song
And cricket calls

Hear me
Hear me hear me
Hear me hear me hear me hear me

If you would just
LISTEN

V.S. Chochezi

Mama ocean beckons

Mama ocean beckons
Whispering lose your shoes
Toss your socks
Let me wash your
Bare and beautiful toes
Let me soothe your woes

I'll tell you fish stories
Full of sand and saltwater
That will fill your dreams
With ocean breezes
Leave sunbeams
In your smile and twinkling
Stars in midnight skies
Behind your sleeping eyes
Mama ocean
Whispers all night
Shouts at high tide
Wakes you with
Wave claps
And foamy, frothy laughs
You rise with rest
In your step
Appreciation in
Your stride
Sand in your hair
Seashells and
Smoothed rocks
In your pockets
Kelp in your teeth
And a new, slower
Steadier rhythm
Like the ebb and flow of warm
Inviting waters on a pristine
Private Caribbean beach
That feels like home

V.S. Chochezi

Special effects

Whoa! Did you see
The wind blow softly
Through the trees
Leaving the leaves trembling
And reflecting sunbeams?

Whoaaaa! Did you see the rainbow
With full spectrum colors
Spanning the whole sky from
One end to the other did you
See the sunrise? It was awesome.

The squirrels in the park
The ducks birds and bees
Moving clouds over head
Grass beneath my feet
The Sacramento River
Rippling through town
The laughing little children
On the playground

These special effects
Often beckon to me
So wondrous, exciting and
They're absolutely free.
Whoaaaaa!

Staajabu

Tree stories

Humans in our ignorance
And arrogance cut down
Trees and make
Paper as if what we
Write, what we have
To say is more important
Than tree stories

Which is perhaps
Understandable especially
Since most of us have
Forgotten how to read
The rings, the bark
The leaves
The still or swaying branches
The buds, the fruit
The nuts, the pines
And yes, of course,
The roots

V.S. Chochezi

Angels camp

Morning early
Foreground sunny
Horizon hazy
Eyes resisting wakefulness

Insistent knocking
Easing from luxurious rest
No tents, tin pots or open
Fire pits on this trip

Nice fireplace comfort
Spa tub jets set

Blinds slip slit open
Searching a golden tinged
Landscape of treetops
Fanned tail flutters from
Window ledge
Knocking continues

Further inspection reveals
Several redheaded woodpeckers
And I wonder, as I often do about
Nature's creatures

Here, surrounded by
Manicured wilderness
With hundreds of trees
In all types of varieties
In red gold and autumn green
Why would woodpeckers
Converge on this building

Pecking balcony and wooden
Trimming, risking injury
They make no noticeable
Progress beyond chipped paint
I imagine their beaks crumpling
Cracking and splitting

In the moment
Wings spread
Black bodies with startling
White patches
Fly by my window
And returning
To the exact same spot
Knocking continues
Joined by a human element
Early morning
Friends at my suite room door
Sleeping in is no longer
An option
Time to write

V.S. Chochezi

Making snow sense

The snow greets me with harsh bright white light
Knowledge of its presence keeps waking me
I rise every few hours to look outside
See if it is still there the glare even at
Night makes me frightful of its power

As this majestic new snow glitters under the
Moonlight star lights street lights blink
Makes my heart skip and flutter as the power
Of this amazing force of wind, snow cold ice
Manifests holding hostages demanding ransom
And sacrifice as people, trees, power lines
And cars crash, clash slip and slide
This unyielding grip of nature's fury is the
Universe's attempt to regain its balance, rhythm
And essential harmony

No emergency, movie, job, quart of milk
Chronic jones, relationship or philosophy
Will outweigh, win out, triumph, trump or beat
This amazing feat as the blizzard reigns supreme.
Three feet of snow has quieted the street
Nothing moves for hours while
Plans and schemes are formulated
Mankind refuses to admit defeat
Children cheer to hear school closings
The snow must have come just for this treat
But there once was an ice age remember?

Staajabu

Early mosaics reflection/meditation

First
Ancient Khemetic symbol of life
Balance between female and male principles
Between heaven and earth blooms a flower

Mirages into an orange
Red flame atop a heavy torch
Beneath a golden
Amber sun immersed
In a calm deep blue sea

Next
Positive affirmations float
In shimmering light collecting
In butterfly's oversized heart
Reflecting shards of truth
Insights projecting our huemanness

Broken glass pieces carefully
Whimsically, instinctively placed
Rejuvenating, renovating
Constructing, resurrecting, breathing
A new being a new beginning anew

Now
To share with following generations
Emerging to revisit, reconnect
With mama ocean just in time

Vibrant and leafy trees hang overhead
Strong brown trunks stand
Alongside tall bright green grass
The moon soon rises within eagle wings

Glad smile of soft rose petals overlap
In the palm of a generous open hand

V.S. Chochezi

Great snack

Farmer's market, grocery store
Back yard garden or roadside stand
Sets the mood for
A ripe and ready peach
Golden and red like a mini sun
Just plucked from the tree
Juicy, plump and divinely scrumptious
Or a tangy deep purple pulpy plum
Dripping with mouth watering flavor
No waxed, preserved, cardboard
Imitations, just a crisp Fuji apple,
Delightfully sweet and sour
Organic yellow pink ruby red grapefruit
And lime green with black seed
Refreshingly cool kiwi
Sweet juicy oranges,
Tangelos and tangerines
Firm yet soft and succulent melons and
A popular favorite, that chunky aromatic
And perfect pineapple
And if you are nodding your head
In the affirmative and it is
Quickly filling with images
Of dark red strawberries
Magical mangoes, beautiful bananas, blueberries
Crisp persimmons, smooth papayas,
Green, red and purple grapes
And mmmm...
Apricots, Asian and Anjou pears, then you
Can truly appreciate the treat
Free of pesticides and growth hormones
So canned, syrupy pre-ripened picked
Packaged and shipped just doesn't compare to
Locally grown seasonal and yummy fresh fruit
Eaten alone, mixed and in pairs.

V.S. Chochezi

Hell no to GMOs...

Real live people need real live food, for real
Real live people need real live food

GMO – genetically modified organism
Genetic synthetic fake food
Please, all the real live people say Hell NO to GMOs

When Frankenstein and his Stepford wives
Entertain Barbie and Ken they may all feast on GMOs but
Hungary burned 1000 acres and banned genetically altered corn

China, Russia and some European countries have
Labeled GMO products for years now
And sources say most corn, beet and soy
Americans eat is poisoned with pesticide-laden GMOs

So shouldn't they at least have a
Surgeon general's warning?
Danger, GMOs may be
Hazardous to your health

In 2012 even Mother Nature
Rejected GMOs destroying
45 percent of GMO crops
Through burning soil
In unparalleled drought conditions

It remains true, you are what you eat
If you don't want to become a
Genetically modified pesticide-ridden organism…

Remember, real live people need real live food
So all the real people say it with attitude…
Hell NO to GMOs!

V.S. Chochezi

Herd of elephants symphony

A herd of elephants stampeded
Through my living room again this morning

Humming a simple tune
They climbed up to the kitchen table
Devoured two bowls of oatmeal
And gulped down a tall glass of soy milk

They trumpeted loudly about the
Glory of a new day
Clanking the kitchen blinds
Then raced into the living room
Hopped up on the sofa
Bounced up and down
A few times and trampled
Through the toy box
Tossing puzzles
Toy cars and crayons
Everywhere

As I timidly opened my
Bedroom door to peer at the
Wild and rowdy creatures
That had taken over my home

I discovered only my wide eyed
Two-year-old grandson who called
Happily, Nani, you're awake!
Wanna play match? (A game we
Used to call concentration.)

Truly a joyous symphony
To these grandmother ears.
Of course I do!

V.S. Chochezi

Renewed acquaintance II

You don't know me and I might
Look deranged to you
Walkin' the way that I walk
Talkin' the way that I talk
Might make me look sort of
Dangerous too, but let me step up kind
Of close and say some things to you
That will make your thought waves come to
Start to jiggle and do, cause a ripple or two
Make you think about the things that'll
Make a man or woman out of you
It ain't killin' your kin or
Having sex just for kicks
It aint stickin' up people so you can get a fix
It ain't wastin' your time watchin' prime time
While they takin' oil out the ground
Destroying trees big time
So they can make planes fly
Make cars whiz by
Make the plants, animals, and people die

Now maybe you don't have a real smooth
Ride or a jacket with your name on it in real cowhide
But you do have time and you got a brain
And if you use them both wisely
You won't have to be ashamed of nothing
You do what you can for your fellow man
And when the chips go down you'll
Always have a winning hand
Protect and respect
Protect and respect
Your parents, your family
Your planet, your body
Your mind, your mind, your mind
And know one thing
If you don't know any other
The Earth is your Mother

Staajabu

Chapter 7

Recognition and Respect

Utambuzi na Heshima

Reconocimiento y Respeto

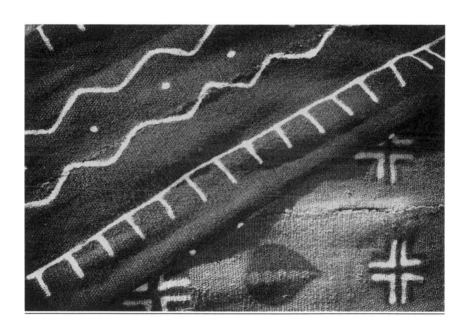

I wish you well

I wish you days full
Of good times and cheer
Wish you true friends
That will always be there
I wish you healthy food to eat
Kind folks to meet
I wish you well

I wish you blue skies
And big shady trees
Wish you good shoes
That don't hurt your feet
Wish you roads without stones
A comfortable home
I wish you well

I wish you songs that
Bring peace to your soul
Wish you live 'til you're
A hundred years old
I wish you luck by the pound
Joy all around
I wish you well

I wish you music that calls you to step
Wish you love, peace and always respect
Wish you work without stress – pure happiness

I wish you well
I wish you well
I wish you well

Staajabu

Mommy look! (for my granddaughter Tisho)

To hear these words from the lips
Of my great-grandchildren warms my soul
Their mommy is young and bold
I remember when she herself was born
And her mommy as well and when she
And her sister were little children
Calling to my daughter, mommy look!

She now mommies her own world with pride
Hide and seek with this one, potty-training that one
Patient and calm; I mean PATIENT
She is the epitome of the word
Bathing, hugging, breastfeeding,
Guiding, correcting, teaching, watching
As her two young ones grow

A new one is on the way as she and husband Billy
Plan and talk and cook and work and
Look mommy, mommy look and
Have you seen the car keys as he bends
Down to give a strong daddy hug and
Gentle kiss to little outstretched arms
Before leaving mommy and babies to
Rituals which give meaning and order to their
Lives as mommies do every day, everywhere

To watch the granddaughter whose
September 26 birth I witnessed during
A hurricane in Dover Delaware
Embrace the role and demonstrate her
Seemingly bottomless energy, skill and mothering
Knowledge with such love and grace is truly miraculous

We wait on the brink of expectation
Makhai, Saje, Billy and Tisho will have
Another addition soon and as with the first two
We will all be better for it.

Staajabu

Far above the surface
You probably also know someone like this

She pens four alarm fire poems
Words show insight, high wisdom
Far above the surface
Where it is too easy to under look

Smoke rises from pages
Fire rages, word flames
Singe your thoughts

She's loquacious
Gregarious in most settings
But her poems lie quietly
Smoldering on pages, in notebooks
On obscure websites, and in anthologies
Tucked away on scant bookshelves

She's wrestled her nerves
And shared her words
Before appreciative crowds at times
And I long to see her stand
Before people again
To spark their spirits
With her young innocent
Wise thoughts

Confident, strong, raw and real
She pens four-alarm fire poems
Extreme wisdom
So far above the surface
Too easy to under look

And if you are privileged
One day you'll experience it firsthand
Feel the intense heat and
Tell tales of how you were singed
And inspired by the blaze.

V.S. Chochezi

When my daughter smiles

It doesn't take much
A sunny day
The kids away
Washing her car
Fixing her lunch
She lights up like a Kinara
Her eyes sparkle
Black onyx in mahogany
She is a stately, elegant
African queen
Lips full, teeth white
And she makes all things
Serene
When my daughter smiles
At me.

Staajabu

Captivated (For Makhai)

His eyes follow me around the room
Wide intense riveted on my every move
He tries to talk to me but
Succeeds only in babbling the sweetest sounds
Certainly a grown woman will ever hear
His demand for my attention beckons me
First grandbaby love completely
Captures my heart

V.S. Chochezi

A beautiful line

She didn't finish seventh grade and became a mother
at the age of 13 but no doubt she had the potential
to be a chemist, carpenter, meteorologist, mathematician,
or artist because she had the cleanest, best looking
laundry in all of Foggy Bottom

She made her own lye soap, mixed just the right amount
of bleach and borax in the wash water and just the right amount
of bluing in the rinse to make our white clothes sparkling white
and if the white clothes were that clean you could rest
assured the other clothes were spotless

An old wringer washer, an old wrought iron
wood burning cook stove, two six-quart boiling pots
a scrub board, two huge zinc tubs three laundry baskets
and a garden hose equipped her back porch laboratory
every Saturday morning right after breakfast
she would already know the temperature, wind direction,
how many loads could be washed and hung by sunset,
and if she had enough clothespins to hang them all

She wiped each clothesline with a rag, checked the
clothes props she had made from scrap pieces
of wood to be sure they would be strong enough to hold
each line, especially the ones with work clothes
whites were hung first, next light colors, then dark
shirts, skirts, pants, socks, underwear, towels, bed linen
and blankets were hung together connected to each other
by clothespins on five lines giving the appearance of dancers
holding hands flapping and frolicking in the breeze

Until I was tall enough to hang clothes, I would play
in the back yard helping to pick up dropped clothespins
pretending the pins were people, listening to grown
folks conversations between her and neighbors
whose yards abutted ours about babies, men, church,
school, the white folks they worked for, what number to play,
dream books, who was sick, who died and Nat King Cole

The women would exchange recipes, offer condolences
or congratulations and more than once I would
hear one of the neighbors comment
when mom had gone inside to check the pots on the stove,
"Grace, sure do hang a beautiful line." "Um hmm"
the others would reply, and I with my clothespin people
sitting in the grass under freshly washed clothes,
would beam with pride and feel very loved

Staajabu

Tribute to reggae - on turning 70

I've seen dreadlocks in moonlight
Felt 96 degrees in the shade
Found love and knew just what to do with it
I've passed the dutchy on the left hand side
Burned down Babylon
Smoked two joints in the morning
Took one draw and was coming in from the cold when
We chased dem crazy baldheads out of town
Had to get up stand up
Stand up for me rights, sang
Redemption song these songs of freedom
So no woman no cry
'Cause the harder they come the harder they fall
And none but ourselves can free our mind
Found that people of the world we are one
That we can stir it up and legalize it
 'Cause I am that I am and Rastafari is
A positive vibration
I've learned some lessons in this life
Seen dreadlocks in moonlight,
Felt 96 degrees in the shade
Found love and knew
Just what to do with it

Staajabu

The griot (for Idu Maduli)

We sit with rapt attention faces all aglow
As the teller's words touch our soul
With detailed descriptions, animated
Enthusiastic and energetic gestures
The magic is woven around us
Drawing us in and making us all a part

We witness spiders, turtles, leopards
Rabbits, birds and elephants come alive
And are amazed at how much they are like us
Teaching and learning helping or betraying through
Truths, tricks, accidents and lies each tale revealing
A hidden attribute, talent, knowledge, common sense
To help overcome obstacles, cope with loss, solve problems

The Griot knows through practice and instinct
What is in each heart for we reveal our inner selves
Through our eyes our acts our mouths
They know what story will suit the crowd and how
Well we will sit still and listen
With rapt attention
Faces all aglow

Staajabu

Dancing with Saleem

When Brotha Saleem and I would dance
At parties and even when I stopped by
His house on 24th Street in Camden
The old school music would flow sweet
The beat connected us and we would jam

He'd spin his wheel chair
And come full 'round on the down
Beat then rockin' his head he'd take
My hand and we would jam

I'd push off do a light skip shuffle out then
Let him gently pull me in and push me
Out again groovin' to the Chilites, Ojays
Blue Magic, Bob Marley, Jazz, funk, R&B

Saleem's contagious love of music
Touched my soul and body
With an ecstasy felt only
When this creative entrepreneurial
 Hustling fast-talkin' impeccably dressed
 Herb smokin', spiritual, crazy, old school
First resurrection Muslim Brotha Saleem Shabazz
Was possessed by the music and
Asked me to dance with him and
Chile we would jaaaaaaam!

May the memory of the laughter and dances we shared
With Brotha Saleem live on in our hearts and minds forever.
RIP Bro. Saleem.

Staajabu

Just musing

There was someone who first
Thought of the piano
Built the first one
Played it first

How sexist to assume
The person was a man
How American to assume
The person was a white man

What a lazy writer
Not to stop the flow of
This poem to search for the
Answer on Google

Not to hand the answers
To the readers to spare them
The process that helped
Create this poem

Never mind that mid-thought
The writer interrupted the
Cacophony of ideas
To consider ah… a poem
Is forming!

To consider pen and paper
To opt for keystrokes and
Computer screen
To struggle to maintain
The thought stream

To nudge you to ride the wave
Sidestroke, glide, flip, backstroke
Along with her

Now imagine the first
Piano player decided
That because he?

Was the first
No one else should
Be allowed to build,
Play or change the piano

No one should be allowed
To create new songs
To be played on the piano
No one should be allowed
To play the piano creator's
Songs either or to revise those songs

Imagine they copyrighted
The piano, patented it for
A hundred years
Did he/she? Lazy writer
To muse and not to google
Right here in the poem

What would Quincy Jones have
Become? Ray Charles? Stevie Wonder?
Mozart? Thelonious Monk?

How many music students
Music teachers, music careers
Would never have existed?

Selfishness? Cornered market?
Smart capitalist venture move?
Hoarding instinct?
Eliminate competition
Or stifle growth, creativity
And future inventiveness
To be the first
The best
The only!

Just musing

V.S. Chochezi

To sisterhood

Sistahs,
Ever feel unappreciated?
Always giving to babies, grandbabies
Lovers, friends, community
Residents and jobs

Nurturing, nursing, listening, advising
Housing, clothing, feeding, loving, even
When it's tough love, giving what is needed
And then some

So much energy flowing…out; are you
Getting an equal amount flowing back in?
Hardly.

While you may feel overwhelmed,
Stressed or even burnt out sometimes
You ALWAYS find just enough energy
Left over in reserves somewhere
To take care of business

To extend yourself to others
To give some more
Give thanks and praises
To the Most High that WE don't need
Endless ego strokes
To motivate us

Because I don't know
About you, but I too
Often feel at the very least
Under-appreciated.
So, thank you for this
Moment to celebrate
With you
To sisterhood
To us!

V.S. Chochezi

Elizabeth Catlett tribute

Daughter of ex-slaves
Woman of my grandmother's
Generation, her art was more
Than an appreciation of beauty
Her heart more than swelled for the aesthetic
Her heart ached and her art served
As social commentary

Reflecting her passion and values
Reflecting her appreciation of Black struggle
Workers and womanhood
She practiced solidarity and chose
Not fleeing, not becoming a fugitive
But a conscientious objector to
A racist America, she opted to
Live the majority de su vida
Painting and sculpting black
And brown gente
Among a rich Mexican terrain

And though she now rests
Among the ancestors
Her creations will undoubtedly
Continue to inspire generations
To express not just for art's sake
But to uplift, honor, respect and
Stand up for justice.

Long live Elizabeth Catlett.
Viva!

Amen and Ashe.

V.S. Chochezi

Rag time

Driven to create
Masterpieces discredited
Labeled undisciplined trash
Untraditional junk

Unaccepted by the mainstream
Pushed underground
Discouraged, depressed
Often relegating the passion
To a side hobby

Developing, growing, creating
With loyal fans and followers
Small lot, the mighty few
Assuring them that they are indeed
The greatest

As they wrestle alone
Aloud
In bars in dark corners
Whispering doubts
Tumbling through the mind
Spilling out sharp shards
Against anyone within earshot

Having that something special
To share with the world
Unable to quite connect
The artist. The philosopher.
Unfulfilled, without life affirming
Acceptance and recognition

The teacher, musician, painter
Dancer, designer, decorator, composer
Chef, inventor, scientist
Longing for stardom

Fame and fortune
Dying sick, penniless

Forgotten or undiscovered
Washed up has been

Languishing in obscurity
Until long after death
The patent is released
The copyright ends

The book is written
The documentary is made
It all gets turned into a movie
Pockets and bellies grow fat

But the artist's family
And community do not prosper
Does the artist/inventor
Genius turn over in the grave?

The song, dance, treatise
Is recreated, translated
And distributed world-wide
Posthumous awards abound

Scott Joplin, just one example
Ragtime perhaps encapsulating
What it means to be
Before your time

V.S. Chochezi

Honoring Chinua Achebe

Courage, culture
Ibo, Africa
Strength,
Life, triumph
Challenge, change
Truth, preservation
Perseverance
Chinua Achebe

Complex, caring
Professor
Survivor, exemplary
Award winning author
Of fiction, poetry
Children's stories
Sharing love for the people

As "Things fall apart"
Nature's cycle continues
Mighty griot joins the ancestors
Leaving us with great memories
Treasures and lessons
The greatest gifts
Knowledge of self
Creative food
For the next generations

Esteemed elder
Accomplished scholar
Literary guru
We remember you
We honor you
Today and always
Chinua Achebe
Ashe.

V.S. Chochezi

Meditation for Maya Angelo (1928 - 2014)

Peace be on you sistah
'Cause you stayed on your job
And on the case
Working for the people
Uplifting the race
Peace be on you sistah

Peace be on you sistah
You made us all so proud
Just to know you and to see you
And we praise your name out loud
Peace be on you sistah

Your work was highly valued
And that's no exaggeration
You truly are the source
Of so much of our inspiration
Peace be on you sistah

Peace be on you Maya, Black Woman
African woman, wife friend poet, daughter
Mother auntie, mentor, warrior queen
Teacher, philosopher, writer, seer
Doer consciousness raiser
Sage, spiritual spirited graceful, generous
Now ancestor, peace be on you,
On yours on ours forever,
Ashe, Amen, Amin

Staajabu

Freedom is never voluntarily given by the oppressor; it must be demanded by the oppressed.
-- "Letter from Birmingham Jail," April 16, 1963

If a man hasn't discovered something he will die for, he isn't fit to live.
-- Speech in Detroit, Michigan on June 23, 1963

Injustice anywhere is a threat to justice everywhere.
-- "Letter from Birmingham Jail," 16 April 1963

Rev. Dr. Martin Luther King, Jr. tribute

He is called a Civil Rights leader
A nonviolent activist and rarely a revolutionary

Why are some publicly labeled Black radicals
Malcolm X/El Hajj Malik El Shabazz
And some called leaders?
Dr. Martin Luther King, Jr.

Semantics or COINTELPRO tactics?
The Black radical nationalist
And the nonviolent protestor
Assassinated like a
Terrorist threat eliminated

But a nation doesn't mourn a terrorist
You can grieve a man gunned down
By a deranged individual
Attempting to avoid martyring
A brave revolutionary
Another conspiracy theory

Rev. Dr. Martin Luther King, Jr.
A Civil Rights leader, nonviolent activist
A revolutionary, a martyr
A man
Amen
Ase/Ashe

V.S. Chochezi

Mzaliwa home

Barely understanding the language
Or the culture, just an outsider observing blind

Admiring the burnt shade of
Their generally lean and tall bodies
Draped in tiny intricate beads
On wire or thread in white and blue, yellow
And orange beads sprinkled amongst and
Intertwined with a show of red

What does it symbolize
This penchant for red?
This clever and skilled beadwork
Adorning their necks, wrists
And head is complemented
By wonderful grades of fabric
Woven with different colors

A smidgeon of black, a bit of yellow
And splashed in brilliant red
Serving as blankets or shawls
They make their homes amid
The plains, reminding me of
Native Americans on reservations

They herd goat and cattle
Living among the giraffe and zebra
They run their own market
They share their wares and
Some of their culture with wazunga
Foreigners or strangers

To all in the land they say
Believe what you will
But East Africa belongs to Massai.

V.S. Chochezi

Mzaliwa = native born person (KiSwahili)

Thanks for the music

Thank you Creator
For your master plan and Pharaoh Sanders
Leon Thomas, Sarah Vaughn, Ruth Brown
James Brown, Motown and the Philly
Sound with the Delphonics
Didn't I blow your mind this time
All over the place thank you
For the temptations, Nat King Cole
Natalie Cole, Cole Porter, John Coltrane
The Four Tops, Rhythm and Blues
BB King, Bobby Blue Bland, Blue Magic
Harold Melvin and the Blue Notes,
Blueberry Hill Fats Domino, King Pleasure
Moody's Mood, Patti Labelle
Phoebe Snow, Ella Fitzgerald, Carmen McRae
D.C. Ray, Ray Charles the Impressions
O'Jays, Funkadelics
The Miracles and Bootsy cause
Music has inspired me
Like Malcolm who was rhythmic
And full of the magic of music as
He spoke in lyrical tones full
Of bass and Marley and Tosh with their
Conscious lyrics sending my head in a dread direction
Give thanks and praises to the Most High
For Miles Davis, Grover Washington
George Benson, Jessie Belvin, Donnie Hathaway
Roberta Flack, positive, Frankie Beverly
We miss you Dinah Washington, Billie Holiday
Minnie Ripperton, Tammi Terrell and Marvin Gaye
Nick Ashford we miss you and for all the inspiration
You sent our way we take this opportunity
To say Asante Sana, Shukran, Muchas Gracias,
Merci and Thank you so very, very much!

Staajabu

Fierce! (For Miles Davis)

Well I was too busy when "Bitches Brew" hit the scene
I mean the album cover was tight with both very light
And very dark Black women in profile along
With Dali-esque renderings of contrasting
Images melding with each other, loud screaming
Colors ocean waves, stars on dark backgrounds
Hooked you at first glance, but I was too busy
Trying to keep it all together
Student, mother, worker, wife, revolutionary,
Finding my way from trying to be cute to finding
Out that cute was the last thing I needed to be.

See I was too busy trying to interpret
The emotions, the non-verbal, the covert
The under-the-covers, undercover the
Opportunistic, egotistical, nonsensical,
Wanna be seen wanna beheardatallcosts
Too busy trying to understand
How they could sit and listen to Jazz when
We had so so so so so so so so so much work to do

I was too busy trying to raise a revolutionary
To pick up where I left off be strong
And know that cute is something you never
Want to be and if people think you are cute
They may take you lightly; they may try to
Manipulate, flatter, mold or recreate you before
You realize cute is the very last thing you want to be
You want to be fierce
You want to be FIERCE
Miles understood that
There was nothing cute about him

Not too busy right now, listening to "Kinda Blue"
Rediscovering anew each cut smooth as butter sounds
Blending, weaving through each other
Fierce!

Staajabu

ABOUT THE AUTHORS

Dr. V.S. Chochezi and Staajabu, the dynamic mother and daughter poetry duo is celebrating their 25th anniversary as Straight Out Scribes. They have shared their work at hundreds of venues around the country and have received several awards for their work. Their poetry has been included in numerous anthologies and various publications. Visit the Scribes website at straightoutscribes.com. Like Straight Out Scribes on Facebook.

V.S. Chochezi, Ed.D resides in Sacramento. She is a part-time college professor. She is an accomplished poet, a mosaic artist, a leadership development trainer, and MBTI practitioner.

Staajabu was born in Philadelphia and raised in Camden, NJ. She is a writer, graphic artist, poet, community activist and organizer.

Straight Out Scribes Written Collections -- many available on Amazon:
- *Mud Cloth Roots*
- *African Reflections*
- *Scribes Rising*
- *Taking Names and Pointing Fingers*
- *This Queendom Come*
- *Bamm!*
- *Crucial Comments and Vicious Verses*

Straight Out Scribes Cds:
- *Priorities (Available on Amazon and at http://straightoutscribes.bandcamp.com/)*
- *Mind Quake*

ABOUT THE PHOTOGRAPHER

Jessicah Ciel has a bachelor's degree in film from CSU Los Angeles and has completed several short films and won awards in film and photography. She is working on a master's in fine arts at Cranbrook University specializing in photography. She is Chochezi's daughter and Staajabu's granddaughter.

Made in the USA
San Bernardino, CA
03 February 2015